THE PSYCHO
SOCCER

by
Massimo Cabrini

published by
REEDSWAIN INC

Library of Congress Cataloging - in - Publication Data

Cabrini, Massimo
 The Psychology of Soccer
Original title Giocare con la testa

ISBN No. 1-890946-25-7
Library of Congress Cataloging Number 99-070333
Copyright © July 1999

This book was originally published by Editoriale Sport Italia, Milan - Italy by Edizioni Correre

All rights reserved. Except for use in a review. The reproduction of utilization of this book in any form or by any electronic, mechanical, or other means, now known or here after inverted, including xerography, photocopying, and recoding, and in any information storage and retrieval system, is forbidden without written permission of the publisher.

Art Direction and Graphic Design
Kimberly N. Bender

Editing and Proofing
Bryan R. Beaver

Translated from Italian by
Maura Modanesi
for REEDSWAIN

Editorial coordination
Marco Marchei

REEDSWAIN INC.
612 Pughtown Road • Spring City, Pennsylvania 19475
1-800-331-5191 • www.reedswain.com

TABLE OF CONTENTS

Introduction iii

Foreword v

Chapter 1 • 6 to 11 Year Old Players 2

Chapter 2 • Teenage Players 21

Chapter 3 • Adult Players 31

Chapter 4 • Senior Players 51

Chapter 5 • Communication 59

Chapter 6 • The Coach 73

Chapter 7 • Parents 103

Chapter 8 • The Referee 108

Chapter 9 • The Club Manager 123

Chapter 10 • Supporters and Spectators 124

INTRODUCTION

In the last few years, life sciences - psychology and pedagogy, in particular - have been focusing great attention on the various problems spreading out in the field of soccer.

This is why I am very pleased to introduce this book, which especially aims at pointing out all the various psychological implications of everyone who is involved in the world of soccer.

Rather than a real psychological or educational treatise, this work by professor Massimo Cabrini is clearly more an instrument for the reader to carefully reflect upon important topical subjects, and can therefore act as a reference for soccer players, coaches, trainers, educators, parents, referees and club managers. It definitely brings out the concept of soccer - which I especially care about - mainly intended as an educational tool and an effective method which helps to shape and develop a perfectly harmonious personality in the young soccer player.

The book concentrates on the various stages of the player's development, from very early childhood to adult age, and also provides the reader with important elements of careful consideration and practical operative suggestions for all those who are involved in youth or adult soccer.

This work can be interpreted as a journey through the various ages of the soccer player, in order to better understand his needs and motivations in all the different stages of his development.

Moreover, in some chapters special emphasis is placed on particular figures who typically play a role of critical importance in soccer, like the coach, the athlete's parents, the referee and the club manager.

I am firmly convinced that those who read this book will find very important and helpful suggestions for further investigation and reflection upon the subject.

> Ermanno Cortis
> *President of the Youth and School Department*
> *of the Italian Soccer Association*

FOREWORD

These pages are intended to provide a journey through the world of all those who are somehow involved in the field of soccer.

I deliberately wrote this book in a journalistic - and therefore popular - style, so as to offer everybody the opportunity for interesting confrontation with the world of psychology applied to soccer.

I also tried to point out some particular ideas for further reflection on the subject, as well as all those problems, doubts and questions which have emerged since I began to address coaches, club managers, teachers and educators while running special courses for both the Italian Soccer Association (F.I.G.C.) and the Italian National Olympic Committee (CONI).

Since I began to run these courses throughout Italy, coaches, club managers, teachers and educators have proved eager and willing to understand and learn more about the various relational problems directly connected to soccer.

While working in direct contact with athletes, I have realized that those who are not directly involved in soccer too often tend to trivialize players' problems, especially in the case of professional athletes. They often forget that, besides being soccer players, they are human beings and therefore have their own feelings, emotions, anxieties and fears like anybody else.

Soccer certainly experienced a great improvement from the qualitative point of view in the 80s and early 90s, particularly thanks to the important progress that science was making in the fields of medicine and biology. Actually, there has been a significant jump forward in the field of soccer conditioning over the last two decades, and soccer players have obviously benefited from such important advances.

Furthermore, I think there will be further improvement and progress in the knowledge and the methods used for athletes' psychological training in the next few years. Today, many coaches rely on the figure of the psychologist to better understand their players and many soccer clubs now include a psychologist in their medical staffs.

Psychology can be very helpful for all of those involved in soccer. It can help parents to make fewer mistakes with their children, trainers and coaches to better know themselves, club managers to understand and become aware of their difficult roles, and referees, spectators and supporters to see the importance of their roles in the sport. This book is intended to be a tool for persuading 'the insiders' and help them understand how psychology can act as a helpful support for all those who are involved in soccer.

I am particularly grateful to all the people I have happened to meet while travelling in the various cities throughout Italy and who have patiently listened. I would also thank all those who - by means of their criticism or complete indifference - have further spurred me to get still more involved in my job so as to constantly improve.

Massimo Cabrini

6 TO 11 YEAR OLD SOCCER PLAYERS

Childhood is the second stage in human life, covering the period between the ages of about six and twelve. It acts as a bridge between infancy and adolescence. This is a critical period of transition when the child's most vital instincts - sexual drive, among others - seem to cool down for a while, thus leaving his dynamic energy to other culturally structured aspects of life, like school and sport. In Freudian psychoanalytic theory, this particular phase in human life is typically defined as the 'latency period' and is generated by the Oedipus complex, which gradually evolves while producing the overall structure of childhood itself.

The evolution of the mother-child-father Oedipal relational triangle and the capacity to handle the emotional strains and the impulses brought about by such a critical situation finally result in childhood.

Throughout the childhood stage, complete peace and quiet seem to reign in the child's instinctual world. Then, a new event of critical importance from the emotional point of view breaks that sort of idyllic peace at about the age of 11 or 12: the pubertal crisis and the beginning of adolescence. Consequently, childhood is a period in human life which develops between these two important events fraught with unknown emotions. This is a crucial period when the child begins to build his own experiences outside the family, shaping and enriching his own personality.

One of the worst errors made by those working in soccer in the past was to consider the young player as an adult in miniature. Consequently, standard training programs and methods typically suggested to adult athletes were erroneously reduced at a quantitative level to be directly applied to youth players. This serious mistake originated from a deep-rooted underlying misconception. Actually, the great difference between the child and the adult player from the qualitative point of view was too often completely neglected.

There is a fundamental aspect to take into account when working with 6 to 11 or 12 year old children: the sport - whatever the discipline - should be suggested to the child as an instrument to gain experience and, therefore, it should be considered as a means, not an end. Consequently, sport means an opportunity for the child to know himself and the world around him, including other human beings, things and objects.

The soccer coach should be familiar with both the physical and psychological features of the child, so as to avoid suggesting an educational coaching plan which does not suitably consider the real abilities of the youth.

The educational intervention on the child should be defined as a well-planned technological intervention based on a proper organization which combines perfect knowledge of the child with the formulation of several hypotheses of work, suitable stimuli, the use of appropriate instruments and methods, a warm psychological atmosphere and careful evaluation at various levels.

Motor development

Children generally enter the world of soccer between the ages of 6 and 11: sometimes because they personally show a particular interest in soccer, or, in other cases, because adults encourage them to get involved in it rather than in another sport. A number of important changes both at the physical and psychological level take place during this critical period in human life.

The motor development of the child between the ages of 6 and 11 is characterized by the development of the individual's capacities to know, understand and improve the use of his body as an instrument for motion. This stage is also characterized by the progressive improvement in the structuring of what is usually referred to as the individual's body image or concept.

The individual's body image is the pattern of all those subjective sensations and feelings concerning one's own body, specifically with respect to the outside world.

One's body image or concept, the awareness of one's own body considered both as a whole and in all its different parts, the ability to perceive and differentiate all the various sensations (stiffness and relaxation, for instance) are the foundations on which the individual can gradually build his motor skills.

Very often coaches working in soccer camps and schools realize that children have serious difficulties in using and moving their feet, almost as if they used them without being aware that they are an integrating part of their bodies. In other cases, 6 or 7 year olds cannot properly perceive their necks: actually, when they need to turn right, they do not use their neck to make their head rotate, but turn their shoulders instead. These are just two of the most common situations which clearly show that the child has not interjected all the various parts of his body yet and, consequently, cannot use them to facilitate movements, since those parts do not exist at all for him.

The improvement in one's body image (or concept) should therefore be a fundamental purpose of primary importance for every individual.

Before drawing up a special coaching plan at the beginning of each season, a respectable coach at the youth level should be able to carefully assess the child's future motor development, so as to plan a suitable coaching-educational method aimed at enhancing those elements the child has not yet acquired. The human figure test is a particularly helpful instrument which is also very simple to use. The child is asked to draw a picture of himself on a piece of paper. By carefully examining the drawing and the presence of a smaller or larger number of body parts, it is possible to better understand which are the segments of the body that have not been 'absorbed' in the mental image the child has built of himself.

It is possible for an individual to improve and refine his body image by means of two different kinds of activity, tonic and kinetic. The term 'tonic activity' includes all those activities connected to breathing and to the discrimination (perception) of the muscle tone.

For the child to improve his body's real life experience, he needs to gradually learn how to recognize the difference in the sensations he perceives when his lungs are filled with air compared to when they are empty. The same can be said about the discrimination of one's muscle tone; as a matter of fact, it is absolutely fundamental for the child to learn how to become aware of and perceive the difference in the sensations he feels when his muscles are contracted compared to when they are completely relaxed.

Between the ages of 6 and 8 in particular, the motor activity of children - whatever the sport they play - should increasingly favor their awareness and knowledge of motion and all the various possibilities that every single movement offers them.

This is why it is particularly important to stimulate their capacities to use all the various basic motor patterns (i.e. jumping, running, crawling, etc.) as well as the postural ones (bending, rotating, lifting movements and so forth). The positive qualities of motion in children are agility, nimbleness and quickness. These are the features that the child develops very intensively over this critical period of life (from the age of 6 to 9).

Aspects such as accuracy, coordination and functionality are other important goals which can and must be developed a few years later, after the age of 10 or 11. Actually, before that period of time, the child is not mature enough to suitably reckon with such critical aspects.

It is fundamental to point out that some physical skills like agility and quickness can be trained and further enhanced with great results after the age of 10. This is why it is necessary to try to work on such features when the individual's structure is still in a favorable condition, which means in a phase of natural predisposition to further improvement.

As to the development of motion in children, the table below shows the main stages in the maturation process.

Table 1
The main stages in the process of motor maturation in children.

- From the age of 5 to 9 or 10: the child learns all the basic patterns of motion
- From the age of 5 to 9: the child enhances the accuracy of his movements
- From the age of 7 to 10: the child enhances his muscle sensibility
- From the age of 7 to 10: the child improves quickness
- From the age of 8 to 10: the child analyzes the speed and the direction of any moving body in relation to his own position
- From the age of 9 to 11: the child finally completes the process of lateralization and further enhances motor-sensorial coordination (eye-hand, eye-foot coordination)

It is fundamental to remember that every individual should be considered in his own independence and individuality. Actually, the suggestions given in table 1 should not be taken literally, since, in reality, we are usually confronted with the problem of either early or delayed development of single individuals.

Just as all the apples on a tree do not ripen on the same day, human beings also have their own individual times for maturation. For this reason, it is especially important to accurately observe and carefully study the group of children which one is working with. This considerably helps to avoid planning one's intervention by taking into account the chronological age of children exclusively, which would be a great mistake. It is obviously advisable and helpful to plan one's intervention in relation to the various age groups, but it is also useful to understand when a child is not mature enough for a certain kind of work or exercise in spite of his chronological age.

Intellectual development

The term 'intelligence' refers to an individual's sphere of thought and intellectual functioning, that is to a wide range of mental abilities and processes, as well as to the individual's capacities to carry out more or less complex actions. This is a wide and difficult concept to define, which implies a number of activities such as perception, learning, reasoning, insight, judgement, memory and so forth.

Intelligent behavior in the human being is mainly based on the possibility of the individual thinking logically, as well as on his capacity to form and combine abstract concepts.

Childhood is a period of critical importance for the intellectual development of the individual, since this period should be considered as a real bridge from infantile thinking to more mature and adult reasoning. This is called formal thinking and is typical of adolescence.

From the age of 6 to 11 the child experiences an important intellectual maturation. Over these crucial years - which Freud typically referred to as the latency period - the child moves in a direction which eventually leads him to develop the capacity to have not only objective interests, but also purely subjective ones.

The child gradually experiences a passage from what is technically defined as preoperatory thought to concrete operatory thought. This will allow him to classify, develop a deeper categorical perception of both space and time and therefore view reality in an increasingly objective manner.

In **Piagetian theory**, the cognitive development in 4 to 8 year old children coincides with the so-called preoperatory stage, that is the phase characterized by intuitive or implicit thinking. During this period, the child's intellectual process is largely dependent upon perceptual features of the world and thinking is intuitive rather than logical (since he does not have real logical awareness yet), although the child is capable of some early forms of symbolic representational thought. During this early stage of life, the individual cannot combine and take into consideration several aspects in one single situation.

As far as soccer is specifically concerned, when a child is playing in possession of the ball and has to challenge an opponent, he is still not able to assess the tactical situation properly: consequently, he cannot suitably evaluate if it is better for him to pass the ball to a teammate or directly dribble past the opponent. Therefore, he will intuitively act following just one of these two possibilities, without considering the positive aspects of the other alternative.

During this period, the child also passes through the so-called phase of egocentricism, which pertains to speech and thought dominated by the child's own internal cognition. The child perceives himself as the center of the world and everything has to move around him. This is why it is difficult to think that a child before the age of 8 or 9 is able to live experiences in terms of a group and therefore fully integrate into the field of team sports disciplines.

Actually, the child will mainly play for himself, for his own pleasure, for his personal success and not for that of the whole team and of his fellow players.

After the age of 9 most children begin to experience, and get more involved in, the sphere of team games, since their way of thinking and reasoning have considerably improved at the qualitative level over this period of time. In reality, children now begin to turn great attention to the group of friends their own age. Consequently, their need for constant praise and approval by others also tends to modify their approach to soccer.

Emotional, affective and social development

Between the age of 6 and 11 the child gradually discovers more and more the world around him. New people are introduced in addition to his parents, who have to this point been his sole influence. He is now involved in different worlds and activities - the school and the game, first of all - which inevitably force him to develop new relationships with other individuals. The teacher in the elementary school now becomes a very important point of reference. The child invests a lot of emotional energy in this relationship, trying to find the elements which could define his own skills and abilities.

In reality, school is the first competitive situation which the child is confronted with, especially in the case of an only child. This situation-competition also brings about the first rewarding and frustrating experiences, which directly affect the individual's self-esteem.

As to affection and emotions, the child now begins to understand that others expect something from him. Very often he wants to be a clever pupil not because he feels that learning is fundamental, but because he would like to ingratiate himself with his parents and the teacher as well, so as to gain their consideration and favor. During this critical period, the experience at school should gradually help the child to become aware of his own skills and possibilities.

When the educational guides - the parents, teacher or coach, in particular - are excessively exacting persons, the child is often likely to develop a sense of weakness and incapacity which will remain so impressed in his mind as to condition his personal behavior in adult age too.

From the age of 6 to 11, the child passes through the so-called latency phase, that is the period of time from the end of the Oedipal period to the beginning of puberty during which both interests and energies are catalyzed by the need of the child to shape his personal identity.

The game, the school and the relationship to other individuals are felt as mirrors which directly reflect the child's real value. During this particular period of his life, the child begins to get involved in sport and very often the emotional and affective components play a crucial role in these activities too.

Youths practicing any sport should be properly understood before being directed and trained. This means that the coach should understand their personal desires and fears as well. The feeling of insecurity and the fear of not being up to the task or inferior to others often encourage the child to break with the sports experience and sometimes give it up completely. This behavior is typically aimed at avoiding any direct confrontation with other individuals, especially those whom the child considers stronger and more skillful than himself.

During this phase of his life, the child's relationship to the same-sex parent becomes increasingly stronger. The child now tends to emulate the same-sexed parent's behavior and the need for his approval is much stronger than the need for the opposite-sex parent's consent.

In general, the same-sex parent is seen as a model, since the child now tends to shape his identity and build up a role which is peculiar to his own sex (sex-role identity).

Shaping one's personality and identity

The personality of an individual is an original, dynamic and relatively stable synthesis of his distinctive ways of acting and being.

Many different factors combine to shape the personality of an individual, including intellectual, motor, motivational, emotional, affective and social elements. In practice, the personality of an individual develops through constant interaction between both individual and environmental factors.

The development of motion during childhood plays a role of critical importance in shaping the personality of the individual. Between the age of 6 to 11, the child enhances his basic and postural motor patterns, which he will use as instruments to develop a deeper relationship with the world around him. Intellectual modifications also become increasingly important. Directional thinking - which refers to the inability to consider different aspects of a situation simultaneously - gradually changes into multi-directional thinking. Also, irreversible thought is progressively replaced by reversible perspective, so that the child is offered the possibility and the capacity to make distinctions and classifications. During this phase in a child's life, thinking becomes less and less self-centered and increasingly logical.

Symbolic games still play a key role over these years, but well-organized play (that is games with set rules) also appear. These are especially represented by the sport-game, through which the child learns how important it is to comply with special rules. During this critical period of his life, the child also gains confidence and self-esteem by directly living a series of new experiences.

Table 2
The main effects of sport on the personality of the individual.

Sport favors:
- *the shaping and the enrichment of one's ego.* By means of greater realistic control over one's drives, sport enhances self-consciousness and encourages the internalization of ideal models, the development and the strengthening of both motor and sensorial capacities as well as greater control over anxiety;
- *greater emotional stability:* in pursuing one's goals and controlling inner emotional conflicts;
- *social integration:* it enhances self-esteem by means of constant identification;
- *the shaping of one's identity and the creation of one's body image:* the identity, defined as the center of one's psychological gravity, is a privileged element in the personality of an individual which is considerably brought out in sport.

Feeling accepted by others, learning and complying with new rules, and identifying with adult models and patterns of life significantly help to shape and enhance one's self-appraisal, an aspect of critical importance in the life of every individual. While being gradually introduced to the outside world the child overcomes his egocentrism and attaches greater importance to the group.

Table 1
Identity.

The identity of an individual involves three different aspects: gender identity, personal-subjective identity and role identity.

Gender identity is one's identity as it is experienced with regard to one's individuality as male or female. It is especially enhanced by the parents by means of both verbal and non-verbal communication. For instance, dressing a little boy in a given way and a little girl in another manner is a clear message which confirms to the little boy or girl his or her own identity. The same is true for the games which are typically played by children: some games are designed specifically for boys, while others are intended for girls exclusively.

Personal-subjective identity is the phenomenological sense that one has of one's own intrinsic self and therefore concerns the realm of psychology. It is gradually built up through the various processes of primary internalization (mother, father, brothers and sisters). The period of one's childhood plays a role of critical importance in the life of an individual, since the relations to other persons gradually help the child to become aware of his own individuality. During these crucial years - and even before, in some cases - reflected opinions of the surrounding environment become an important standard by which the individual judges himself.

Role identity is the third component of every individual's identity and represents the external parameter of one's personality. It is a sort of social dress in constant conflict between one's desire to conform with the behaviors and attitudes of one's role in life as it is associated with one's sex and with one's personal unconscious needs. By playing different roles, every individual takes an active part in the social world. By absorbing and accepting values, standards, attitudes and rules as one's own, the individual acts so as to make that world become subjectively real (Berger and Lukerman). The way in which an individual perceives the people around him is not based on reality, but on a particular picture of the reality in which the other person is typically recognized (role).

Every sports activity with an educational intent obviously affects the development of the individual in a very positive manner. Actually, special training for motor skills helps to make children independent. By practicing sport, children can often gain confidence and enhance their self-esteem, especially if they can also experience success. The reinforcement of the child's identity occurs through his relationship to the adult, who is supposed to encourage and bring out the advances and successes of the young player. The desire to develop a shapely and harmonious body during adolescence is considerably rewarded by sports activity, especially in boys. Of course, female teenagers are still faced with the stereotype of female identity represented by supermodels and movie stars. Fortunately, the figure of the high profile female athlete is becoming more and more popular. It is extremely important for teenagers to play a role in the group of friends their own age, and sport can considerably help them in this. As a matter of fact, during this critical period of life, sports-motor activity allows the youth to enhance his self-esteem and gain confidence in his own skills and possibilities. It also encourages him to constantly seek improvement, by showing the way of sacrifice and strong will as a fundamental means to achieve his goals.

Learning in childhood

Several subjective conditions concerning all the various areas of the individual's personality and many different objective conditions connected to external situations and inputs combine together to contribute to the learning process in every individual. The most typical and common learning processes are: imitation, conditioned reflex (or response), trial-and-error, intuition and learning by understanding.

Imitation or modeling learning is very common in childhood. As a matter of fact, children tend to imitate, copy and intentionally model their actions and behaviors on those of adult people, especially if adults are perceived as models for their own identification. In some cases these adults are not physically present in the child's life, such as TV and sports stars, but are nevertheless powerfully influential. In light of these considerations, if the soccer coach is approached and perceived positively by the child, the imitation learning process is very likely to be particularly effective and successful. This is especially true as far as ball technique is concerned, but also affects the way one speaks, dresses and behaves in general. This also helps us to understand that the coach bears full moral responsibility in his relationship to the young player. This kind of learning process requires no reinforcement, which means that no repeated, or reinforced, occurrences are needed to improve learning.

Conditioned reflex (or response) learning involves the use of both reward (positive reinforcement) and punishment (negative reinforcement). Through this kind of learning process the individual is directly conditioned to behave properly. Nevertheless, this behavior is not really advisable for this particular age group in the field of sport.

Trial-and-error learning. This is undoubtedly the most important learning process in soccer. Actually, the child gradually learns how to improve his technical movements and performances by increasingly reducing his mistakes and bad attitudes, so as to slowly approach the right model (the ideal model) more and more. In order to keep it simpler, I would say that this is the typical behavior representative of the saying 'Practice makes perfect...!'. It is important to underline that the coach plays a role of critical importance in this kind of learning process, since he takes an active part in correcting any possible mistake or wrong behavior. As a matter of fact, corrections should be made in an ideal psychological atmosphere.

Intuitive learning is the most immediate and direct among all the various kinds of learning processes. The light is suddenly turned on in our mind (sudden revelation) so that we are immediately offered the solution to a problem which had been worrying us for a long time. In reality, intuition results from a very quick mental processing of schemes, patterns, data and memories which are finally combined together in a perfect way.

Learning by understanding (or explicit learning). This kind of learning process takes place consciously and is typically based on reasoning, on the individual's ability to process data coming from his personal experiences and stimuli. Conscious learning especially suits young players after the age of 8 or 9 and becomes increasingly frequent as the developmental process of the individual evolves. By contrast, it is much more difficult before that age since the child still perceives the reality in a partially restricted manner (concrete thinking) in that period of his life (concrete operatory stage).

Motivation

Motivation is the energy, the desire, an intervening process or an inner state that impels or drives the individual to satisfy his own needs. The human being struggles to satisfy several needs: from the basic, primary drives - connected to one's need to survive - to behavioral, psychosocial and more cultural drives, directly connected to one's need for self-realization and fulfillment of one's potential.

Each age group has its own needs and, consequently, its own typical motivations. From the age of 6 to 11, the child usually tries to carry out various motivational aspects by means of playful motor activities. The little boy or girl is generally driven to action by motivations basically connected to his body in motion and motivations directly concerning both his emotional and affective satisfaction as well.

Table 3
Need hierarchy according to the American psychologist A.H. Maslow

NEED FOR SELF-ACTUALIZATION:
self-fulfillment, realization of potential
ESTEEM NEEDS:
achievement, prestige, status, self-esteem
BELONGINGNESS AND LOVE NEEDS:
affiliation, love, acceptance, private life
SAFETY NEEDS:
freedom from threat, security, safety, protection
COGNITIVE NEEDS:
sex, activity, exploration, manipulation, curiosity, knowledge, understanding
BASIC PHYSIOLOGICAL NEEDS:
food, water, air, temperature maintenance, pain avoidance, rest

Motivations are psychological, physiological and cognitive drives which direct the behavior of the individual towards specific goals. While living many different experiences, the child learns how to distinguish pleasing sensations from unpleasant ones at a kinesthetic, emotional and affective level, and also learns that his relationship to other individuals is mediated by his personal motivations. Moreover, the child constantly looks for confrontation with other individuals, as well as for identification with his peers and slowly learns to internalize and comply with rules.

While outside influences are fundamental for the child's motivations, his individual relationship to himself also plays a role of great value in this context. The child wants to constantly prove to himself and also rejoice when he understands he can finally achieve his goals. Moreover, if adults also help him - which means by avoiding excessively demanding or impossible requests which would be out of his personal reach - the child gradually enhances his self-esteem and gains confidence.

In general, a 7 year old, a teen-ager or an adult play the same game, but everyone specifically looks for the personal satisfaction of the typical needs peculiar to one's developmental stage in the same playful experience.

Specific motivations to sports activity in childhood

Between the ages of 8 and 11, special motivations to sports activities in general are usually divided in two separate groups, which include primary motivations (which derive from basic needs and are assumed to be common to all the members of a particular group) and secondary motivations (or acquired drive).

Primary motivations: play and competition. As far as the individual in the so-called developmental age is concerned, primary motivations include motivation to playful activity and competition as well.

Play can be considered as the main motor activity in the life of a child. As a matter of fact, while playing the child also learns to gradually know himself, as well as the world and the people around him.

Play is an activity with no specific goals: it is a funny and enjoyable reality, characterized by a playful idea, which is finally defined in its objective content and in the assignment of social roles (Hahn). Undoubtedly, this is the most important experience in the life of every individual, since it is especially aimed at stimulating the motor, intellectual, emotional and affective development of the child. Every individual at any age considerably benefits from playful activity.

In the very early years of his life, the child is mainly involved in motor-sensorial play. This particular kind of playful activity allows the child to grasp a number of elements directly connected to the reality of both people and things around him and to cause and effect relations in general. Furthermore, it also helps the child to know how to use his body from the point of view of motion.

While growing up, the child gradually shifts from motor-sensorial playful activity to symbolic play (games of make-believe and fantasy). Through this particular kind of play the child learns how to transfer the elements of his personal imagination to the things and people around him and, in some cases, directly to himself. For a child of this age, a common box of matches can easily become a car, or a boat, or an island. Through symbolic play, the child discovers how to play several particular roles: he plays at being a stationmaster, a doctor, at keeping shop and therefore at 'keeping the accounts' and so on. He does this from a purely imaginative point of view, by means of common situations which typically belong to the world of adults.

Later on, organized play is finally introduced. All the games based on specific rules, which the individual must comply with, cannot develop but within a set plan. *The main features of this kind of play are:* gratuitousness, delimitation in both time and space, and pleasure due to a release of emotional tension (Huizinga).

In his playful activity, the very young soccer player combines both symbolic aspects (for instance, he imagines himself to be his favorite player) and elements which typically concern organized play with set rules. As a matter of fact, any playful sports activity during this particular stage is a real game with rules, which requires the child to comply with specific rules and interdictions included in the laws of the game.

Play is an element of crucial importance in the growth of every child. If the child cannot give enough free play to his playful nature, the full development of his personality will certainly be somehow more difficult. Many studies on this subject have proven that the lack of possibilities for the child to play freely can even bring about significant retardation in both intellectual and emotional development. A clear example is that of children growing up in orphanages. Their environment often lacks the stimuli to encourage playful activities and as a result are more likely to suffer from intellectual deficiencies later in life. For the young player to achieve a high level of psychological maturation, Orlik and Botteril heartily suggest:
1) the constant changing of roles and positions, so as to discourage specialization;
2) to avoid any automatic internalization of any athletic movement;
3) to remove any excessive emotional and environmental stress in youth sports competitions;
4) to avoid and discourage any sharp criticism to young players and between them;

5) to generously reinforce and encourage positive behaviors;
6) to constantly dissuade parents from expecting something impossible from their children or making unreasonable demands on them.

Consequently, motor activity in soccer too should take this important reality into proper account and therefore have purely healthy and playful nature and goals.

The competitive nature of sport is an important motivation which will be further discussed in the chapter focused on adolescence. Competition during childhood is of great importance, since it allows the child to compete and measure his strength with other individuals of the same age. Through competition, he gradually learns how to cope with confrontation and deal with both success and defeat.

During this phase of his life, it is particularly important for the child to draw successful conclusions from his confrontations with other individuals so as to find positive confirmation of his real value. Consequently, it is advisable to avoid suggesting excessively demanding competitive situations in which the child would be regularly defeated and would therefore lose self-confidence. Nevertheless, it is also fundamental for the child to discover that losing is a part of life and something to learn from. Donít forget,however, that successful experiences play a role of critical importance in enhancing his self-esteem.

Secondary motivations: motivation to affiliation and motivation to self-actualization. Motivations to both affiliation and self-actualization especially characterize this particular age group.

Motivation to affiliation is the need for companionship, association and cooperation, the need to be loved by other individuals, be part of a group and have one's personal space and role in it. This stage is particularly evident starting from the age of 9 or 10 onwards.

The child slowly learns to not play only for himself, but to look for cooperation, support and approval by other individuals of the same age. This passage from pure egocentrism (a self-centered perspective) to sociocentrism (a definitely wider perspective) is key in soccer whether intended both as a sports discipline or just a playful activity.

The child gradually learns how to experience play from the point of view of mutual cooperation and the success of the team becomes a personal goal. The reality was completely different before. Even though the child played with other people, in practice it was as if he played alone. When he returned home after a game, he didn't generally tell whether the team had won or lost, but only remembered what directly concerned him (the number of goals he scored during the match and so forth).

Motivation to self-actualization or success - the need to fulfill one's potential - directly combines with the personal drive to competition at this age, which was discussed above.

In late childhood, the child feels an increasingly strong need to have his value confirmed by others. This is exactly the period when a good part of one's personality is strongly shaped. If both parents encourage independence, appreciate the success of the child and are not excessively demanding as to their child's performance in sport, the sports experience can bring about positive results and play an active role in enhancing the child's self-esteem and therefore shape his identity.

Too often, children who are unsure of themselves and fear confrontation and competition with other individuals tend to recoil from any sports experience, since it is usually perceived as an event causing anxiety. This usually happens because they feel a strong inner need to play well and be successful and this is the obvious result of the education they have received over the years.

The ball and the development of the child

The never-ending success, popularity and charm of soccer are certainly connected to the use of that very common but absolutely indispensable tool called a ball.

Games played with a ball date back to very ancient times, which proves that the human being has always found great satisfaction for playful motivation by means of this very common object.

The child generally sees the ball very early in his life and immediately 'falls in love with it'. The ball soon becomes a real playmate, through which the child gradually learns to discover himself, the people and the world around him.

History of the ball. The ball has been used since very ancient times and, consequently, it is almost impossible to perfectly ascertain the period when it was first used as an instrument in sports and games.

The main reasons for the incredible success of the ball - intended as an instrument of amusement - should be probably attributed to the dynamics which inevitably result from its shape and instability.

The ball was considered the symbol of either the sun or the moon god among some ancient peoples living in South America. Due to its spherical shape, it was considered the perfect form, or better, as the symbol of perfection.

The Greeks would play with special balls coated with leather and stuffed with feathers. They often inflated the bladder of animals. The external part of the bladder was sometimes covered with strips of cloth and padded with horsehair. The Greeks played several ball games; one of the most popular was very similar to modern volleyball. Another typical game was *trigona*, which involved the players positioning themselves in a triangle and throwing the ball to each other. *Episciro* was played by two opposite teams, while *urania* involved the players throwing the ball as high as possible.

The Romans played the same games but gave them different names. They called the ball *pila*, but if it was padded with feathers it was called *paganica* - from 'pagus' (which means 'village'), because it was mainly used in the countryside at the beginning. If the ball was smaller and inflated, it was generally named *follis* or *folliculus*.

The Roman *harpastum*, which corresponded to the Greek *episciro*, was played with a ball stuffed with cloth and involved the players either kicking or throwing it around. It was a very tough and highly athletic game which was very similar to modern soccer. In one of his most popular dialogues, Lucian reported that the players were all beaten up and bleeding at the end of the game. *Harpastum* was the game that legionaries liked most, probably because of its tough nature. Actually, legionaries were the ones responsible for spreading this kind of play around in the farthest provinces.

The main virtues of the ball were also praised by Claudius Galen (129 to 201 AD), the greatest physician in ancient times after Hypocrites. He suggested that everybody play games with the ball and warmly extolled the healthy and therapeutical value of ball playing in his most popular work 'Ars medica'.

Ball games were also played during even the worst periods of the decline of the Roman Empire.

The High Middle Ages was a period of darkness for most ball games and in fact they disappeared almost completely. The only game with the ball which was reported in those ages was played in Great Britain. Originating in Brittany, it crossed the English Channel and spread out in Great Britain. It gradually became so violent and tough that players even died in some cases. The ball was covered with leather and two teams contended for possession; they were even allowed to come to blows in order to take the ball from their opponents and win possession. Each team had to fight to take the ball from the opposition and carry it as a trophy to their own town. Since towns were generally very far from each other, the winner could change several times, and each time there was a brutally tough fight for the trophy. This particular game survived in Great Britain until 1819, when the British authorities were forced to ban it due to the increasingly frequent bloodshed.

In the Renaissance, a new ball game spread out in Florence which was very similar to the Roman *harpastum* and was consequently called '*Florentine harpastum*'. In his famous work 'De Orbe' written in 1516, Pietro Martini d'Anghiera spoke about that game which was played with a rubber ball - a substance which was actually introduced in Europe after the discovery of America. Modern soccer somehow originated from that game, the so-called *Florentine harpastum*. In the same period, a new ball game began to spread out France: it was named *jeu de paume* and practically corresponded to the original Italian tennis, of which Antonio Scaino wrote in 1555. The game was a match between two teams who had to throw the ball over a rope which divided the field in half. Original tennis (paume) enjoyed great popularity. The game became a real professional sports discipline in a very short time and the thousands of spectators who watched tennis matches were often relentless gamblers.

Modern soccer actually originated from the Florentine harpastum which was played in Florence because that game involved the players struggling for the so-called 'wind ball', whose weight was about ten ounces and which could be either kicked or struck with the fists by the two teams made up of 27 players each. Even so, in light of these observations, we could say that Florentine harpastum was more similar to something like rugby than to modern soccer.

Ball and body. By using the ball the child gradually learns to discover and know his body better. He would like to control the movements of the ball and direct it wherever he wants. Consequently, while expressing his intent as to his relation to the ball, the child considerably enhances his perception of all the various parts of his body.

Touching, kicking, holding and throwing the ball are all basic important movements which help the child to slowly become aware - in an increasingly resolute and clear manner - of the parts of his body which are directly involved in carrying out such playful activities (his hands, feet, neck and so forth).

Furthermore, through his direct contact with the ball, the child will gradually learn how to distinguish different body sensations, such as muscle contraction and extension and, more importantly, he will also discover his perceptions connected to inspiration and expiration. The coach should obviously play an active part in this important process by constantly offering the child new stimuli in the playful activity. The movements of the ball and its bounces will certainly become further important stimuli in the motor learning process, since the child will inevitably tend to copy and reproduce such movements.

Between the age of 6 to 8, the ball should enhance:
- foot-eye coordination

- hand-eye coordination
- space and time coordination
- the development of the overall body framework (feet, head, hands, neck, etc.)
- the perception of both strength and speed.

The child perceives the ball as a real extension of his body. The ball can get to the places where he cannot go and his desire to constantly discover something new as well as his curiosity can be totally satisfied by means of this tool.

Ball and affective investment. It is proven that the child tends to invest in the ball great affection and emotions. Some psychoanalysts firmly argue that the ball is a real transactional symbol of the mother's breast and therefore a substitute, much like a baby's pacifier. In fact, the ball receives a clear emotional and affective investment by the child.

The child does not content himself with an ordinary ball: he wants his own ball and usually tends to do everything possible to identify it immediately, by personalizing it with a special mark or his name, for instance. In the child's relationship to other individuals, the ball becomes one of the main instruments of socialization and helps him to develop new relationships in the common playful experience. While playing with the ball, the child confirms and enhances his identity, gradually learns how to reward and satisfy himself, and discovers the desire and the need for constant improvement. Both the ball itself and the instance of possessing it can significantly reassure the child, since they make him feel important and popular.

The ball has great and immediate attraction for adults, too; this consequently means that it also helps to make communication and interpersonal interaction between adult and child much easier.

As was previously pointed out, the child invests such a lot of emotional and affective energy in the ball at this stage of his life that he obviously becomes possessive of it. Consequently, passing the ball (which means giving the ball to another person) is felt as a deed of gift, which generally occurs only once the child has developed a positive relationship with his fellow players.

The ball: speech and mutual communication. While playing with the ball, the child also develops his language ability and favors mutual communication. Verbal language is considerably enriched as the child learns new words and progressively shifts from linguistic egocentrism to a new open verbal perspective.

The coach should be able to carefully observe the child playing, understand and finally interpret non-verbal communication, that is all the aspects of communication that are expressed without the use of the overt, spoken language and emerge in the child's relation to the playful activity.

The ball can be handled, thrown and kicked in many different ways (with great accuracy, with kindness or in full anger); each of them obviously implies a specific hidden message that the educator should be able to grasp and interpret successfully.

The ball slowly leads the child to open up to new individuals as possible playmates, thus favoring mutual communication and the development of new relationships. The way in which the child communicates with the people around him is an important instrument for him to express his inner condition and experiences (both positive and negative). Non-verbal language still plays a role of critical importance in the overall process of communication between the age of 6 and 8. The way in which the child approaches the game and playful activity in general are particularly rich in non-verbal linguistic content. Information about feelings and emotions (that is any situation of fear, joy, doubt and hesitation) in the child's relationship to other individuals is mainly communicated through the body by way of gesturing.

TEENAGE PLAYERS

Adolescence is undoubtedly the most difficult phase in the overall developmental history of every young athlete. In the period between the age of 11 to the attainment of physiological and psychological maturity, the personality of the young athlete is characterized by constant conflict and contradiction. As a matter of fact, conflict and contradiction especially emerge in sport - and in a very dramatic way, in some cases. The sense of uneasiness and anxiety which are typical of adolescence are the direct consequence of the developmental stage which the individual is passing through, as well as of both psychological and physiological transformations which characterize his journey to complete maturity.

The teenager feels that he is no longer a child, but sometimes still likes and cannot avoid being a child. At the same time, he is longing to be an adult, without unfortunately being aware of what maturity really means, since he has no experience of life at all. Consequently, he is constantly living in a state of uncontrollable anxiety, since he fails to shape his identity completely. Unfortunately, this violent and impatient need of the teenager to become an adult is in constant conflict with the real time it takes for the maturation process to develop completely - and this time is often very long. This situation is dramatically distressing for the youth, especially when he has to face confrontation with individuals who are of the same age, but are experiencing premature development.

The individual nature of both physiological and psychological development - which can involve either premature or late maturation - inevitably results in situations of total uneasiness which emotionally affect every aspect of the individual's life in the critical developmental age: actually, the teenager fails to shape, define or even understand his personal identity.

The teenager's personality is nothing but a confused, upset and often contradictory identity, combining both the past (the firm convictions of one's child experience) and the future (the ideal model of adulthood), but with no real and reassuring present. The teenager finds it very difficult and almost impossible to answer the persistent question: 'Who am I...?'.

Intellectual development

All the various intellectual changes which characterize adolescence (which means starting from about the age of 11, in general) are of critical importance both from the qualitative and quantitative point of view. The complete development and the final awareness of formal logical thinking - the so-called formal operatory stage, characterized by hypothetical and deductive cognitive functioning, combined with the consequent ability to deduct intellectual hypotheses, often stimulate the young soccer player to perceive himself as if in a condition of unlimited power, thus encouraging him to severely oppose adults. The teenager can no longer accept that 'adults' decide for him and feels - often wrongly - that he is able to handle problems and choices of crucial importance.

The youth is frequently in conflict with adults and is often in bitter conflict with his educator or coach. He may disagree with the coach's technical and tactical solutions or may not accept the positions on the playing field which he considers unsuitable for himself.

The previously docile and obedient child can rapidly become a rebel and therefore oppose established rules and laws.

It is obvious that the development of the so-called hypothetical-deductive cognitive process also brings about positive effects on the soccer performance. As a matter of fact, the youth can now delay his motor response (passing the ball, for instance) until he has finally hypothesized and carefully assessed the optimum solution. This successful transformation is of crucial importance, since it determines the possibility for the athlete to choose the ideal tactical solution only after conscious and rational thinking. This was not possible in childhood, since motor response was more instinctive and immediate rather than logical.

Emotional and affective development

From the point of view of feelings and emotions, youths in their teens typically tend to search for the security of their own identity. The strong need for total independence generally causes the teenager to develop a sort of intense love-hate relationship with adults. He is prone to attack adult figures in general, and to copy and emulate them at the same time (identification process).

The term 'identification' actually refers to a mental operation whereby one attributes to oneself, either consciously or sub-consciously, the characteristics, the behaviors, and the thoughts of another person or group. The notion of transference is key in this context: one emotionally lives other people's experiences as one's own, which obviously involves the passing on, displacing or transferring of emotions or affective attitudes from one person onto another.

Since the youth fails to completely feel at ease in the role of an adult, this generally drives him to behave as if depending on somebody else. This behavior of intentional dependence is typical of the previous developmental stage and therefore puzzles the adults around him. The fear of not deserving respect and consideration combined with very low self-esteem may drive the teenager to live the soccer experience as a possible way to shape and refine his real value in absolute terms.

Moreover, the fear of cutting a poor figure may stimulate him to apply all his energies to the soccer experience, although the opposite may also occur. In some cases, the youth may even prefer to escape in order to avoid the sense of frustration deriving from possible failure, which would mortally hurt his self-esteem. This clearly explains the high percentage of desertions from soccer in this particular age group.

Another previously unknown reality suddenly appears in the emotional and affective life of teenagers: the opposite sex. As a matter of fact, in this period the boys slowly begin to develop new contacts and relationships with the girls and this very frequently brings about a state of anxiety and fear. Feeling the pleasure of the opposite sex and receiving a successful reply in this sense inevitably enhances one's self-esteem and confidence in a very positive manner. By contrast, any failure or lack of positive confirmation is very likely to cause feelings of insecurity.

In this critical period of his life, the youth can even perceive any affective and emotional involvement so dramatically that his psychological energy can be absorbed completely in the situation. Furthermore, the lack of proper and suitable sex education directly affects the development of the individual, especially if one is already prone to anxiety. This especially applies to boys, who often live their sexual relationship as an instrument to assert their strength, power and virility.

Body and motor development

The body of the young teenager gradually changes both inside and outside. Hormone maturation - and all the physiological and psychological consequences and drives that it typically brings about - stimulates the youth to approach and discover the opposite sex and, as was already pointed out, the fear of not being properly appreciated by the other person is key in this context. This is why playing soccer can be seen as a helpful way to attract attention to oneself.

The success or failure in one's first experience with the opposite sex can either encourage self-confidence or enhance anxiety for fear of not being handsome or up to the situation.

Both premature and late development can cause serious problems for the individual. In particular, in the case of delayed puberty in boys, the late bloomer often finds it difficult to be at ease among his friends whose male adult sexual attributes have already developed. As a matter of fact, body hair, male voice and genital development are felt as a dramatically distressing desire for him in this situation. In this case, it is fundamental to reassure the boy and help him to understand that everyone has his own maturation time. Physiological transformations and changes in one's height are not often homogeneous and harmonious. Sudden growth can frequently affect performance and, in particular, coordination (space and time coordination). It is proven that some important acquired skills - like heading or volleying - are very likely to be temporarily impaired, since it takes more time for the mind to recreate the body image and consequently restore the original coordination balance. This can further raise in the youth the fear of suddenly becoming unable and not up to the situation, which obviously makes him shrink from any sports experience.

The group

The teenager perceives others as mirrors which directly reflect his personal value. He constantly looks for either positive confirmation or unsuccessful denial of his value in all the people around him. As far as the soccer experience in particular is concerned, his soccer teammates generally enhance his desire to achieve team goals and plans and stimulate cooperation - but this is possible only if there is no bitter rivalry between them.

It is considerably rewarding for the teenager to successfully find his position inside the group and be accepted and loved by his teammates, since this makes him feel important in the community. By contrast, if envy and competition eat into the soccer team, the youth may feel the need to belong to another more reassuring group, which is usually referred to as 'the group of one's peers'. This group is completely detached from and independent of the soccer experience, is generally made up of people of the same age and can therefore help the youth to feel well integrated, since all the members share common problems and difficulties.

The group of his peers helps the teenager to realize that his friends also share his personal problems. Consequently, he feels understood by others, since they all speak the same language. Unfortunately, the group of one's peers can sometimes become an obstacle to sport, especially when most friends - or even all of them - do not play soccer. If the group of one's peers generally give great importance to sport - as a result of special values which are deep-rooted inside the community - the teenage athlete is further encouraged to get involved in soccer, since this may eventually become a helpful weapon to gain more popularity among the people of his own age.

Motivations to sport during adolescence

Motivation to sport plays a role of critical importance during adolescence. Actually, many youths shrink away from any sports in this particular period of their lives. This sort of escape consequently results in the phenomenon of desertion, which is typical of this age. In order to avoid many youths in their teens abandoning all sports activity, it is fundamental for adults to know and understand the needs and the motivations that the teenager would like to satisfy through sport. While dealing with the motivations peculiar to adolescence we will divide them in two separate categories (as we have already done while discussing motivations in childhood): they involve primary motivations (play and competition) and secondary motivations (motivation to success, affiliation, aesthetics and compensation).

Primary motivations: play and competition

Play. We already discussed this subject in the chapter especially dedicated to childhood. Certainly, the playful activity plays a role of great importance in the sports experience of the youth during adolescence, too. Unfortunately, the need to plunge oneself into a completely fictitious reality - which is typical of play - is not always satisfied in one's sports experience, especially in the case of competitive sport.

The teenage soccer player generally discovers in the game the possibility to relieve mental strain stored up during the course of the day. If the youth lives the playful activity in total serenity, this cannot but favor creativity. As a matter of fact, it definitely enhances divergent thinking, thinking that is characterized by a process of 'moving away' in various directions and typically yields brilliant ideas and solutions. For soccer to be a really exciting experience, it obviously needs full creativeness and players who can successfully find brilliant, creative, personal and alternative solutions. Unfortunately, a typical behavior which heavily penalizes individual creativeness too often prevails in the mentality of most soccer coaches; training sessions are frequently monotonous and repetitive, the ball is used very little and, consequently, the youth cannot really enjoy training.

Indulgence towards error is also extremely important in this context. There are too many youths who are terrified at the idea of missing a pass or a shot while playing soccer. This generally occurs when the coach, and even the parents in some cases, are excessively severe in their criticism.

As Tumin used to point out, play and creativity are a mainly aesthetic experience.

The fear of being criticized, disappointing general expectations or even losing his place in the team usually drives the teenager to expose himself to danger as little as possible, thus avoiding possible mistakes and failure. This is why he will gradually get accustomed to playing in the simplest way possible: he will pass the ball to the most immediate teammate, won't run the risk of taking a dangerous shot and won't ever exploit his potential thoroughly. In this way, he will never become a top-class creative player.

Competition. So much has been written on competition. Basically, it is possible to distinguish two separate schools of thought that handle the subject in two contrasting ways.

One school of thought states that competition - at any level, and especially during the developmental period - is absolutely negative. Negative because it is supposed to be an instrument for the strongest to crush and overcome the weakest, thus favoring the creation of a definite hierarchy of values among a community of people.

By contrast, the second school of thought - which is in favor of competition - points out that the concept of competition in sport simply reflects the competitive spirit that is inborn and deep-rooted in our society. Briefly, the reality of sport is nothing but a faithful reproduction of our social reality and, since the sports activity is one of the multiple cultural expressions of our social environment, competition must exist in sport, too. Like in most situations, also in this case the truth probably lies in the combination of both philosophical currents.

Competition is one of the very few lawful means that our society approves and allows one to vent aggressiveness, which is proven to be the real propellant in any competition.

This element is of great importance for the individual to restore both psychological and physical balance because it is demonstrated that keeping too high a level of aggressiveness and mental strain inside oneself inevitably brings about a wide range of both mental and bodily illness - which are typically referred to as 'psychosomatic disorders' - in the long term. It is true that winning at all costs too often becomes a real limitless obsession, but it is also true that individual competitive behavior directly mirrors one's personality and characteristic way of behaving, thinking, feeling, reacting and so forth.

In conclusion, we are firmly convinced that for a positive and helpful approach to competition to be possible, the young athlete should be constantly trained to consider his opponent not as an enemy to defeat, but as a mirror reflecting both his strengths and weaknesses. Lawful and healthy competitive spirit should encourage the athlete to perceive the competition as fruitful confrontation, and not as pure struggle where 'my living implies your dying' is the only important reality. It is practically impossible to conceive of a sport with no competitive component at all, since we are actually living in a basically individualistic society where everybody struggles to create one's own space, too often to the prejudice of somebody else. For further details, read the table 'Competition and aggressiveness' on page 28.

Secondary motivations: motivation to success, affiliation, aesthetics and compensation.

Secondary motivations are also commonly called personality factors, since they are the practical expression of the history, the experiences, the real life and the education of every individual.

Motivation to success. It is that particular drive which allows the young athlete to interpret and live his personal sports experience with great involvement and determination. Those who are especially motivated from this point of view generally have a strong will to constantly enhance their performances and their untiring involvement in training is aimed at their personal improvement. In this case, the athlete cannot accept his 'poor skills' and limitations and therefore reacts by throwing himself heart and soul into his activity, trying not to overlook any aspect in order to successfully overcome his weaknesses. This type of athlete - especially if he is also particular skillful - can often achieve great results and successful goals simply because he never gives up his strong will to constantly improve.

This is exactly the case of the young soccer player who constantly wants to perfect his passing or heading skills and all those technical movements which he considers to be very poor (either right or left footed passes, for instance) by means of special training directly on the playing field, maybe in total solitude after the usual conditioning session with the whole team.

While carefully studying top-class champions in various sports, some researchers have found that those athletes who were especially motivated to success had been brought up in a particular way by their parents. Actually, they discovered that the parents of those athletes had always tried to encourage full independence in their children and inculcate them with the desire to work hard and do everything possible to achieve their goals.

Furthermore, those parents had also been able to bring out and properly appreciate the efforts and the results of their children. This clearly helps us to understand that for young athletes to be positively motivated to success, parents should not behave as fanatical supporters of their children, but should leave them free to live their personal sports experiences in total peace and serenity.

Motivation to affiliation. The need for affiliation is particularly strong in the individual during adolescence. As a matter of fact, the group of one's

Table 2
Competitive spirit and aggressiveness

Aggressiveness is the mainspring of competition. In the human being, it results from the combination of inborn systems of purely instinctual nature and mainly culturally acquired systems. Some state that aggressive behavior directly results from pure instinct, while others believe that it is brought about by a non positive relationship to the surrounding environment. Today, we are generally more inclined to think that aggressiveness is qualitatively connected to specific situations; this is why we can easily distinguish different kinds of aggressive behavior.

Aggressiveness is typically considered as a potential of our nervous system, which makes use of philogenetically-inherited structures. Nevertheless, these close 'patterns' would not be enough to bring about aggressive behaviors. For such mechanisms to be activated, they must be connected to particular relational, social and learning events. This means that there must be an external situation which is processed by the cerebral cortex (the most cultural part in the brain), which promptly conveys such a particular emotional meaning to the event that it immediately needs an aggressive response. Such immediate response is activated in the remotest area of the brain which lies in the limbic system.

Competition in our society is the mature, constructive and creative manifestation of aggressiveness especially aimed at the final self-actualization of the individual (Salvini). Repressing or neglecting one's aggressiveness may upset one's psychological balance, thus causing serious neurotic disorders.

Sport is undoubtedly one of the very few situations where one can 'freely' express one's aggressiveness without being punished by society.

Parents too often educate their children to repress any form of aggressive behavior, thus favoring their unconscious natural disposition to vent this particular kind of energy towards themselves. In this way, they unintentionally lay the bases for the development of several psychosomatic disorders. Many athletes who seem to lack grit have been educated to inhibit their aggressiveness; consequently, they cannot serenely abandon to competitive spirit even in their sports behavior. Their deep-rooted sense of guilt and fear to hurt the opponent may sometimes prevent them from living sport in total freedom and therefore hinder their self-actualization.

peers (the people of one's own age) - especially if it corresponds to the team - can considerably encourage one's personal commitment and involvement. The youth actually feels the need to be appreciated, integrated and eventually identified as a member of that particular group. This definitely favors motivation to affiliation, since taking an active part in sports also satisfies the youth from the emotional and affective point of view.

Aesthetic motivation. There are many athletes who feel a strong inner need to carry out and show highly harmonious, fine and accurate technical movements. In soccer, there has always been great confusion on the subject, since those who naturally look for and take pleasure in performing refined technical moves are generally branded as 'individualists'.

It is true that the constant pursuit of over-refined technique often has a mainly self-centered purpose, especially among youths; nevertheless, there are also athletes who consider the aesthetic aspect as the ultimate object of their sports experience.

Aesthetic motivation and creativeness also have many important traits in common. Unfortunately, we cannot but realize that most of these significant aspects are too often repressed by education, starting from a very tender age.

Motivation to compensation. Now, we would like to focus the attention on personal redemption. The history of sport clearly teaches us that the mainspring in the pursuit of success at all costs is often released to counterbalance and react to particular situations of psychological, social and even physical suffering.

Some particular situations when one has experienced dramatic feelings of inferiority - at any level - can consequently stimulate the desire to take one's revenge in sport. In these cases, the sports becomes the main instrument for the individual to redeem himself, improve his existence, feel normal and similar to his peers. But unfortunately, the change in general condition that sport can sometimes bring about cannot always perfectly match with a real transformation in personality; consequently, a top-class athlete - who inevitably becomes a former champion at the end of his brilliant career - too often returns to his original reality of 'social outcasting'.

The relationship with the coach

Like any other adult figure, the coach is generally perceived and approached in an ambivalent manner by the young teenager. Consequently, the coach should be able to develop a strong relationship with the youth which is based on his personal authority, but excludes any form of authoritarianism.

A competent coach is sensitive enough to properly understand the feelings and the emotions of the teenager by also interpreting his non-verbal language. In particular, the coach should identify in each youth those personal motivations which could be satisfied through sport. If the coach is not up to this task - which means that he is unable to understand the athlete - the relationship will be particularly difficult and various problems will develop.

Teenage athletes are often likely to project on to their coach typical situations of conflict which inevitably result from difficult relations within their families.

A competent coach cannot fall into the trap of personal emotions; this means that it is advisable for him to avoid feeling or getting involved personally. The young teenager generally attacks the role which the coach is playing inside the group, that is his role of educator which is naturally invested with special power. It is obvious that the teenager's aggressiveness towards his coach is a clear symptom of the difficulty of the youth to approach and bear confrontation with a superior authority. Such critical problems may also develop in the teenager's relationship to other adult figures, like teachers and professors, for instance. Mutual dialogue and communication is key in this context; obviously, the more the coach is able to communicate with his athletes, making them feel highly responsible, the more their soccer experience will have significant formative influences on every aspect of their personalities.

ADULT PLAYERS

In the last few years, soccer has become more and more scientific in constantly pursuing the possibility of further improving soccer players' performances. Today, both sports medicine and the theory of training are combining together and are therefore play an integral part in the conditioning of modern soccer players. In the last few years, the psychological aspects are also spreading out in a field where athletes are constantly being asked more and more - even though this important science is still approached with a certain mistrust.

A psychological approach to the soccer player definitely allows the coach to unveil and deal with problems of critical importance, since it helps to consider and use human resources in a much better way, so that they can be put at the disposal of the whole team. Such crucial problems as anxiety, psychological training, motivation and the successful handling of interpersonal relationships inside the team-group are a positive starting point for the coach to help every single player to express and fulfill his personal potential with no psychological restraint.

However, it is fundamental to point out that psychology cannot make players without talent become top-class players or champions, but can considerably help talented players to fully exploit their skills and potential.

The importance of knowing oneself/Self-knowledge

Personal motivation to get involved in a sport often acts as a stimulus for the individual to gradually get to know oneself better. All those who have played soccer - at a certain level, obviously - have soon realized that one's individual reaction to competition is inevitably conditioned by one's physical and psychological condition.

When the athlete is faced with hard training and disappointing situations, sooner or later he will begin to wonder about the meaning and the real importance of his soccer experience. In particular, he will wonder why his performance on the playing field is often influenced by his physical and mental state. The very first answers can be found in his understanding and knowing some basic aspects of crucial importance which especially concern nutrition, sleep habits and so forth. In reality, the athlete is inevitably trained to know his body better. The reality is somehow different as far as basic psychological factors are concerned, since we have never been culturally trained to give great importance to such details.

Nevertheless, there are many athletes who, thanks to their strong passion for soccer, are further motivated and therefore encouraged to ask themselves questions, thus trying to know and understand themselves better. I would like to underline that these athletes would have never wondered about themselves if they had not felt such great passion for soccer.

In some particular moments of one's life, it is extremely important to stop and seriously think about oneself in order to understand where one is going, what one's main goals are, whether they are realistic and whether they really correspond to one's identity and desires. Such important thoughts often emerge too late, when personal motivations are waning. Furthermore, such considerations are very unlikely to develop in those who are finally achieving great success, or the goals they had previously set. In reality, one typically dwells upon the meaning of one's life and generally plunges into such a reflection when one is passing through a particularly hard period or when one's personal goals have already been achieved.

As far as soccer is concerned, in general it is possible to say that a player is much more likely to wonder about what he is looking for when he has already been involved in the world of soccer for some time. The life of a professional player is not as easy as it is generally perceived to be; it is a highly particular existence, which is obviously remunerated very generously, but which should not be described in trivial or oversimplified terms.

Professional players should be able to make sacrifices and give up many things. For instance, living far from their original home inevitably brings about serious problems and difficulties. Developing new relationships and living a new social life is not always so easy, also because the so-called new 'friends' they meet wherever they go often prove to be mere acquaintances who typically approach the athlete simply because he is a popular person. In fact, it is not so difficult to find professional players who complain that they have lived negative experiences regarding their friendships; this is due to the fact that most of those relationships were lived with a manipulative approach by those who pretended to be friends, but only tried to personally benefit from the player's popularity and wealth.

Groupies, or hangers-on, permeate the world of the professional soccer player and others in positions of fame and wealth. The professional soccer player must choose his associations warily and can never be entirely sure of the intentions of others. As his popularity gradually fades and his career comes to an end, he may find himself alone, no longer of interest or use to so-called friends.

In some particular fields of their lives - especially as far as the realm of affection and emotions is concerned - professional soccer players generally have more difficulties and run more risks.

Popularity involves a number of serious problems for professional athletes. The press is always ready to carefully investigate their behavior and words so as to cause scandals, while even damaging the interpersonal relationships of the players themselves. Psychological stress is very difficult to handle and obviously has serious consequences for the athlete both at a physical and psychological level. From this point of view, it is evident that professional players are living in a highly demanding reality today.

In conclusion, it is clear that a player who can look inside himself and carefully reflect before making important choices cannot neglect such relevant aspects in order to avoid underestimating the consequences he has to face to achieve certain goals. These significant problems frequently emerge at the psychotherapist's, where an increasingly large number of soccer players go when they finally understand they need psychological support to successfully handle the difficulties of their lives.

For the therapy to be effective, the athlete - and not the club - should personally choose his psychologist; when the psychotherapist works with the whole team it is often more difficult for some athletes to let themselves go in a totally intimate and confidential relationship with the doctor. They often fear that what they tell may be used against them; this is why it is much easier and more helpful for them to let themselves go in a relationship with a psychologist who is completely detached from the reality of their team.

Motivation in adults

For adult soccer players to get maximum benefit from their personal sports experiences, it is fundamental that they be perfectly aware of their motivation. According to professor Martens, athletes' motivations can be typically divided in two different categories: intrinsic motivations and extrinsic motivations.

Intrinsic motivations. Intrinsically motivated athletes feel a strong inner need to do everything they can to exploit their potential to the utmost, constantly improve and achieve great success mainly intended as the final achievement of the goals they had previously set.

Intrinsically motivated players typically get from their success in sport important elements of gratification and personal fulfillment, which are mainly connected to their personalities (intrinsic motivations actually refer to motivations of any behavior that are dependent on factors which are internal in origin and do not stem from external rewards). Hard work and the final achievement of much longed-for targets are rewarding factors which the athlete includes in the ideal model he has built for himself.

Achieving great success in sport - like in any other field of their lives where they want to compete - is an important instrument for such athletes to find personal satisfaction.

Professional players who can get considerable enjoyment while playing soccer and always work hard without sparing themselves, generally feel a very deep and strong intrinsic motivation.

In general, intrinsically motivated athletes play neither for money nor for other kinds of satisfaction dependent upon external factors; they naturally throw themselves heart and soul into sport and get personal gratification simply because they know they always do everything possible and try their utmost. Intrinsically motivated players who feel an intense need for success and achievement are not generally inclined to lose all interest in sport when they have achieved significant goals.

Final satisfaction does not generally belong to the personality of such soccer players. Even at the age of 35 they will still be highly motivated to work hard and try their utmost, thus constantly pursuing self-fulfillment. They feel a strong need to train and play well and always do their best in any situation. Any coach would like to have this type of athlete in his team because he does not need to be regularly motivated and encouraged; furthermore, he can act as a model for the whole group and therefore stimulate his teammates.

Extrinsic motivations. An athlete who is constantly stimulated by strong extrinsic motivations is undoubtedly much weaker than an intrinsically motivated player from the point of view of his character and personality. This particular type of athlete considers sport as an instrument, a means to get personal material, social and psychological confirmation and appreciation from the outside world.

Behavior that is motivated by rewards and/or punishments administered by outside forces is extrinsically determined, and success, winning, money and popularity are the main rewards that such athletes search for through sport. Consequently, these persons are naturally highly dependent on the surrounding environment. These players need to be constantly encouraged by means of increasingly rich rewards, since they easily achieve final satisfaction.

Extrinsically motivated athletes usually feel personal commitment as an instrument to achieve their goals. In reality, strenuous exercise and fatigue during training are much harder to bear for these players than for intrinsically motivated athletes.

Moreover, extrinsically motivated athletes typically find it difficult to handle personal frustration, re-appraisal and reproaches; they often abandon sports activity once they get final satisfaction or when external rewards are no longer stimulating for them.

Psychological training

An increasingly large number of athletes now commonly speak of mental stress, psychological breakdown, fear of winning and success, feeling of despondency, lack of motivation, lapses of concentration, etc. as typical feelings and conditions which often impair their performances. It would not be so difficult to quote a number of examples to perfectly describe these common situations, which seem to prove that there is a sort of 'magic factor' that negatively affects and inhibits the athlete's performance.

Modern athletes generally train and work harder than in the past, but they cannot always achieve those successful results in the competition which they may expect according to both the quality and the quantity of increasingly innovative conditioning methods. In reality, the previously mentioned 'magic factor' - which is nothing but the psychological component - plays a key role in sport and very often tricks athletes; this is why modern training plans tend to focus greater attention on the importance of psychological factors. In the last few years, experts have tried to understand and identify the main aspects which one is supposed to deal with in order to better train the mind of the athlete to handle all the various problems and difficulties of competition.

Stress, concentration, motivation and all the factors which generally bring about a state of anxiety are certainly the main elements on which athletes' psychological training should be specifically focused.

It is fundamental to realize and understand that for an athlete to be highly competitive, not only should he work hard at the physical level to train his muscles, but also work so as to create such favorable psychological conditions which enhance his performance during the competition. For this to be possible, modern conditioning schedules for each athlete should obviously also include special mental training plans, so as to focus suitable attention on the psychological aspect. Psychological training should not be considered as something standardized which is suitable for everyone, but should be personalized, which means accurately studied and planned according to the personal reality and condition of every single athlete.

In order to avoid any possible lack of motivation or a serious psychological breakdown, it is advisable at the beginning of the soccer season for every athlete to set specific goals which he will try to achieve over that period and therefore accurately plan his personal soccer season. Remember that it is fundamental to set realistic - not purely Utopian - targets, which must be directly connected to the individual reality of every single athlete.

When we speak of setting personal goals, we do not generally mean winning a match. We specifically refer to the athlete's improvement according to particular physical, technical, psychological and relational parameters. This means that every athlete should first carefully identify those target parameters which best suit his personality and try to achieve such goals during the course of the season, while also determining both the quality and the quantity of work and exercise he is going to carry out to reach such purposes.

As far as the psychological field is specifically concerned, the analysis of one's personal season planning should be based on the accurate investigation and evaluation of one's personal past experiences. Consequently, an athlete should carefully assess and identify all the psychological aspects which brought about serious problems or difficulties in the previous season. Different athletes are likely to identify different problems, like feelings of anxiety, lack of concentration, lack of motivation and so forth. In light of this personal analysis, every athlete will set special individual goals for the approaching new season.

Among all the various important goals that athletes try to achieve by means of special psychological training, concentration is undoubtedly a key problem in any sport. Being particularly attentive and concentrated means applying one's mind and focusing one's effort exclusively and intensely on a particular task at a certain level of competence and for a set time.

When one decides to face a situation or set a task, the performance - whatever its level - inevitably requires the individual to focus great attention on it.

When the athlete is particularly careful and alert, he can successfully concentrate on the task he is carrying out and nothing can distract his attention. He can immediately see and hear what he is doing and can also perceive all the sensations deriving from his body; to some extent, he is also able to read the level of psychological and physical concentration on the faces and bodies of the people around him, both teammates and opponents.

Concentration is not something inborn, but is an important ability which can be gradually trained and enhanced. In reality, every athlete should first learn what to turn his attention to, when to pay greater attention to something and how to keep maximum concentration in some particular situations. Attention obviously implies the ability to select among a number of different stimuli. There are some particular moments when a soccer player should turn his attention to the outside: his passing, shooting, dribbling movements and so forth; while, on other occasions, he needs to especially focus his attention inside himself in order to understand and analyze the sensations that his body is conveying: heartbeat, breathing, muscle sensations and so on, so as to carefully assess his personal condition and therefore plan and handle his performance accordingly.

Stress

Soccer, too, should be analyzed and considered as a combination of many different situations, some of which have particularly stressful effects. The conditioning session and training stimuli as well are real stressful events, for instance, which are clearly aimed at gradually shaping and enhancing the athlete's capacity to stand the final stress: the competition.

For many years now, sports physiology has been studying all the effects of physical workloads on athletic success. By contrast, sports psychology specifically focuses the attention on all the various emotional, affective and social events which may act as stressful causal agents, thus affecting the athlete's performance. Those involved in soccer know that such emotional agents can often influence the performance significantly. Each player attaches a certain importance and a particular personal meaning to the match and his individual emotional condition cannot but vary accordingly. The match is frequently experienced and felt as something uncomfortable and with increasing apprehension by a number of players who can express their sense of uneasiness in many different ways.

Some athletes have mainly psychological problems, while others generally suffer more from organic disorders in the period immediately preceding the match. Both psychological and physical problems basically originate from the athlete's inner condition, the way he considers and approaches the match and from his general soccer experience as well.

According to the Austrian-born Canadian endocrinologist and psychologist Hans Selye, stress is a non-specific response of the body to any disturbing external agent (forces or pressures). As a matter of fact, as this psychologist clearly pointed out, the human body can stand stressful events and agents through the so-called general adaptation syndrome (GAS), which is actually responsible for protecting the body against severe stress and any situation that it perceives as something dangerous. General adaptation syndrome implies serious nervous and endocrine mechanisms and activities which consequently prepare the body for either a defense or an attack reaction.

The body's general adaptation syndrome develops in three main stages:
  1) alarm reaction - characterized by two sub-stages: a shock phase

and a counter-shock phase - (adrenal stimulus is very intense and the production of corticosteroids is heavily enhanced);
2) resistance stage - the recuperative process continues and the body is ready to react against the stress;
3) exhaustion - exhaustion ensues if the stress is too severe or prolonged.

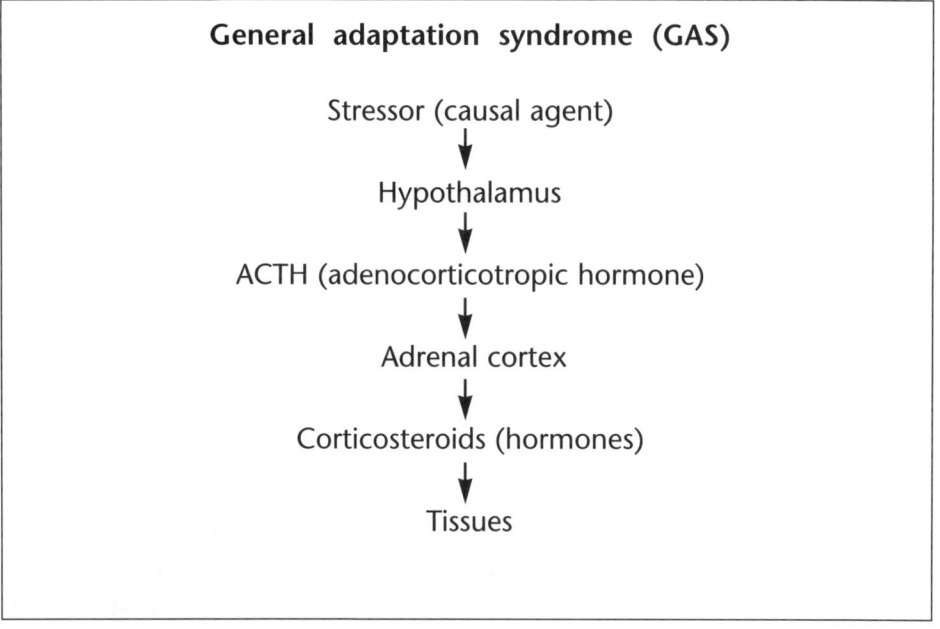

It is fundamental to consider both internal and external factors in the working mechanism of the adaptation syndrome.

Amongst *internal factors*, I would like to especially focus the attention on:
- accelerated heart rate,
- accelerated breathing,
- sudden acceleration in reaction (response) times,
- muscle tone increases,
- increase in blood sugar and oxygen concentrations.

External factors - that is those factors which can easily be noticed from the outside - include among others:
- labored respiration,
- excessive sweating,
- sudden blushes.

Prolonged stress can sometimes bring about serious pathologies like headaches, kidney disorders, ulcers, gastrointestinal disorders, rheumatalgia, hypertension, coronary diseases and even cancer formation in some particular cases, as professor Fornari suggests.

Table 4
Main events directly connected to severe stress.

Family
- the loss of a loved one (wife, husband, child and so forth).

Work
- an excess of responsibilities
- pressing rhythms of work and bitter competition
- an excess of concentration
- conflicts with those who give orders
- disaffection and alienation
- unhealthy place of work.

Others
- apprehension about one's body
- hurry and impatience
- low self-esteem.

When speaking of stress, we should remember that the 'stressor' (that is the causal agent) should always be considered from two different points of view. As a matter of fact, both the quality of the stressful agent and the way the individual feels and handles such stress are of critical importance. The same causal agent (stressor) can bring about different reactions according to the individual's personal condition.

Feelings and emotions, as well as self-esteem, self-confidence and one's general psychological and physical condition can significantly influence - and therefore either enhance or lower - the effect of the causal stressing agent on the individual.

Anxiety

Anxiety is a psychological experience, a vague, unpleasant emotional and affective state with qualities of apprehension, dread, distress and uneasiness that everybody has felt at one time or another. It often develops on those occasions when we are faced with a particular situation that we fear we are unable to handle successfully.

Anxiety can result in a general state of mental strain, accelerated heart rate or profuse sweating. Every single individual expresses his own anxiety symptoms through absolutely personal manifestations. Such symptoms are generally likely to appear before taking an examination, when one has to meet an important person or in many other common situations which inevitably bring about a state of apprehension connected to the fear of failing to be as one really would like to be. At that moment, stress considerably increases and hundreds of doubts and fears upset our minds. In particular, our psychological energies are catalyzed by our bursting need to find out new strategies which are finally aimed at achieving what we really want and long for.

But what is the meaning of, and the reason for, all this?... Basically, both in sport and in life in general, the human being is constantly trying to improve his knowledge of and get control over the reality around him. In particular, he wants to know and control whatever attracts him most; the more unsure he is, the more spasmodic his desire to control the reality becomes.

When one desires to achieve a particular goal and is highly motivated, he struggles and does his best to build a suitable path towards that specific target. He will accurately plan and do everything possible to reach the final result and his dream will become true in his desire to personally smooth his path to the ultimate goal. However, he will undoubtedly have to deal with problems and difficulties, which may result both from his personal feelings of insecurity - like lack of self-confidence and under estimation of his skills and possibilities, for instance - and from external objective situations which cannot be directly controlled by the individual. This is why a state of anxiety typically develops, which basically reflects the inner condition of the athlete who fears not to be up to the task and fail in his intent.

The growing sense of anxiety which typically appears before a match is probably the most serious psychological problem which athletes in general - and soccer players, in particular - have to regularly deal with.

Soccer players are constantly under pressure. They are perfectly aware that the level of their individual performances directly reflects their real values and that their skills are inevitably judged accordingly.

Supporters, club managers, the press and even the teammates can be perceived and considered as real judges by the soccer player. Athletes know that the world of sport is utterly ruthless and even the smallest thing is enough to break any friendly and confident relationship with the outer world; this often enhances in players the fear of failure.

What I would like to underline is that the general sense of anxiety that players generally feel before a match is not so different from the feeling that students typically experience before taking an examination. As a matter of fact, it is not sport that usually triggers off possible anxiety reactions, but it is the way we personally feel and live sport that can bring about such an unpleasant state of uneasiness.

This generally happens when we are highly motivated to achieve our goals. A player does not necessarily feel the same sense of anxiety and does not experience the same violent reaction at all matches. It is obvious that the feeling of anxiety will be further enhanced when the athlete is going to face a particularly important and determinant match.

There is another significant aspect to consider, which is directly connected to the athlete's personality. Before being an athlete a player is undoubtedly a person and the origin of his anxiety should first be discovered and understood in his real identity as an individual. The more unsure the person is of himself, the lower his self-confidence and the more a constant component of general anxiety - better known as 'trait anxiety' - is likely to develop. In general, it is possible to state that the more an individual has a strong personality, is trustful and self-confident, the less he is inclined to suffer from feelings of anxiety and consequent unpleasant reactions in his life.

However, it is obvious that the surrounding environment may also bring about or enhance general states of anxiety and this particularly occurs when the player feels he has to bear excessive responsibility. In youth soccer in particular, young players are often very likely to develop general anxiety disorders and reactions when their parents are exaggeratedly involved in their children's sports experiences.

If the young soccer player considers his sports activity as an instrument to win his parents' love and attention, his need to work hard and try his best during the games may even reach negative levels of tension and anxiety, thus inhibiting the possibility to freely express and fulfill his real potential. How can an individual manifest his inner sense of anxiety, in practice? Anxiety is nothing but a psychological condition which inevitably tends to involve and affect the physiological, behavioral and psychological components as well.

Physiological aspects. They synthesize and represent the condition which can be objectively perceived in a typically anxious person.

The human body shows a number of different signals and symptoms indicating a general state of anxiety and the most typical and common manifestations are:
- labored breathing,
- increased heart rate,
- trembling and muscular spasms,
- abnormal bursts of heat and cold,
- severe sweating,
- nausea and gastric disorders,
- diarrhea,
- frequent and precipitant urination,

- mouth and throat feeling dry.

Every player develops his own particular anxiety syndrome and, consequently, everyone has and recognizes his own peculiar symptoms.

Behavioral aspects. When one is faced with a situation which brings about a growing sense of anxiety and cannot overcome such difficult conditions, he can adopt some particular defensive behaviors - which also exist in the animal kingdom - every time he feels that danger is impending. Taking to flight (avoidance response) is the first possible solution and the desire to escape inevitably causes the individual to go off his set targets from the psychological point of view, at least.

Consequently, the athlete will warm up very lazily before the match and will think about the strength of the opposition and the difficulties that he is going to deal with rather than about his psychological concentration. Sometimes, he will also complain of his feeling sick (stomachache, headache and so on). In youth soccer, young players are often even likely to give up the game completely as an immediate way to escape from a situation which they consider as something excessively dangerous.

Immobility is the second kind of reaction to anxiety. When a player adopts this defensive behavior, he will typically become rigid and contracted, his face will appear almost expressionless and his eyes will stare into space. He will feel as if paralyzed with tension and will move and act almost as a 'zombie' without being aware of what is happening around him.

Psychological aspects. A state of intense anxiety generally causes significant modifications in the individual's normal mental activity. A player who suffers from anxiety typically feels dramatically unsure of himself and finds it difficult to concentrate and choose a definite competitive strategy. Great confusion lies in his mind: many different thoughts and memories gather together, thus impairing his perceptive skills, so that he finally perceives the reality around him as if it were filtered through a lens which negatively affects events and situations, while also magnifying problems and difficulties.

As was already pointed out, it is important to speak of real anxiety syndrome and we need to remember that symptoms are highly personal and therefore peculiar to every single individual. As a matter of fact, two equally anxious athletes may suffer from completely different symptoms; some may express their sense of anxiety at a physical level while, in other cases, anxiety may affect the individual's behavioral and psychological components.

Another significant distinction is directly connected to the personal awareness of the particular kind of anxiety one is suffering from. When we feel a sense of anxiety in many common situations of our lives (in sport, in our interpersonal relationships, at work and so forth), we should refer to trait (or behavioral) anxiety. By contrast, when great anxiety only develops in some particular situations, we typically suffer from temporary state anxiety which is connected to specific environmental stimuli. But does anxiety always have a totally negative connotation? The real problem is not that anxiety does exist as a common feeling and condition; the key point which finally helps us to understand whether anxiety has serious inhibiting effects on the athlete's performance is the way the athlete perceives and handles such feelings.

It is proven that all athletes do not negatively perceive those pre-match physical and psychological sensations which frequently cause anxiety and apprehension in other players and seriously impair their performances. There are some athletes who can perceive and interpret physical and psychological tension as a positive signal which their bodies use to communicate that they are preparing to try their best - a process which is commonly known as 'activation' (preparing for action) in psychology.

Activation is a sort of general excitement which makes the brain more or less reactive and ready to absorb and process information and stimuli so as to produce suitable responses This type of athlete is all geared up and excitedly ready to face the match as soon as he perceives such sensations. By contrast, the other type of athlete - who is undoubtedly weaker from the psychological point of view - generally lives such feelings and sensations in a negative manner: he immediately gets frightened and discouraged and only attaches to such sensations an exclusively negative connotation in relation to the final competition.

When the very first symptoms of anxiety (increased heart rate, shortness of breath, trembling, muscular spasms and so forth) appear, they immediately think: "Here I am again, I am anxious once again, I cannot try my best...". The real problem of psychologically weak athletes is that most of their energies are absorbed by their strong need to keep such unpleasant sensations under constant control. In this way they inevitably take part of their energies off their main goal (the match), thus practically impairing the efficiency of their competitive performances.

Suggestions to fight anxiety

Anxiety is a psychopathological disorder which is too often trivialized and neglected. Until some years ago, the so-called pharmacological approach was considered the only effective method to relieve anxiety disorders in our culture. Today, too many doctors are still prescribing anti-anxiety drugs to those patients who show typical anxiety symptoms, thus neglecting all those effective psychological treatments or innovative therapies.

It is advisable to underline that psychoactive substances and drugs can only relieve pain and the symptoms of most anxiety disorders, they cannot change the reasons and psychic causes from which anxiety essentially originates.

In this chapter we are not going to deal with the common pharmacological treatments typically administered to relieve anxiety disorders - and that are not recommended to athletes in general - rather, we will focus the attention on all those innovative psychotherapeutic techniques which have become increasingly popular in the last few years. They include: autogenic training, Jacobson's progressive relaxation techniques, biofeedback, yoga, Zen Buddhism meditation, musicotherapy, analytic psychotherapeutic procedures, hypnosis and other relaxation techniques.

These innovative techniques and alternative solutions are all aimed at relieving and controlling tensions and some of them also aim at enhancing the inner growth of the individual to remove the original causes of most anxiety disorders.

Athletes can gradually learn how to use such alternative psychotherapeutic techniques through accurate training with the help of a competent psychologist. Once the athlete has perfectly understood and learned the new technique, he can easily use it either to support standard conditioning methods or in those particular situations which regularly bring about intense anxiety.

Autogenic training. This is undoubtedly the most common and well-known form of psychotherapy. It consists of two distinct levels: the inferior level and the superior one.

The so-called inferior cycle includes six main workouts: body weight, body temperature (heat), heart rate, breathing, solar plexus and forehead temperature.

In general, it takes about three to four months to learn this relaxation technique and the learning schedule usually implies one session a week (thirty minutes long, in general) with a competent psychologist who typically applies Schulz's standard technique. Autogenic training is generally more suitable for particularly persevering people. This relaxation method is aimed at reaching a state of passive concentration which applies to personal imagination. At the beginning it is not always so easy to accept the key concept of 'thinking of doing nothing', but the patient can gain control over his anxiety disorders as learning gradually improves.

Autogenic training is a helpful technique which can be learned and improved both individually and in a group setting.

Jacobson's progressive relaxation technique. In its original form this technique includes a wide range of exercises which are specifically aimed at helping the individual to perceive his muscle tone. In practice, the individual learns how to relax muscle groups one at a time, the assumption being that muscular relaxation is effective in favoring emotional relaxation. While learning this technique the patient also learns how to distinguish the different sensations of contraction and decontraction in his muscle groups.

The complete treatment is very long and generally lasts more than one year. For the therapy to be really effective, the athlete should practice one hour a day and attend special psychotherapeutic sessions with a competent psychologist for a total of about one to three hours a week.

This is a particularly difficult technique to learn and apply and is specifically recommended to those who consider sport as the main purpose in their lives and are therefore highly motivated to improve from any point of view. Innovative and alternative solutions have gradually developed from the original technique. In general, these variations are all aimed at accelerating the learning process.

Biofeedback therapy. This is a therapeutic training technique used in the USA which enables the individual to control and modify - within certain limits, of course - his functioning and, in particular, involuntary and automatic biological functions like blood pressure, heart rate, muscle tension and so forth.

Learning takes place by means of a machine which is connected to special sensors placed on some specific areas of the body. If one wants to refer to the parameter of muscle tension, such detecting sensors are placed on forehead muscles. They convey a special signal to the central machine which, in turn, gives out another signal showing the individualís muscle tension level through a special acoustic or illuminated visual device.

Therapeutic training teaches the individual how to modify such parameters and bodily functions through proper relaxation.

Unlike all the other techniques, biofeedback therapy allows the patient to keep the effects of relaxation under constant control both visually and acoustically.

Yoga and Zen meditation. Rather than essentially therapeutic relaxation techniques, both yoga and Zen meditation should be considered as real philosophies of life. In reality, there are many athletes who currently practice yoga in all its different forms and have succeeded in gaining control over their minds, senses and bodies, thus enhancing both physical and mental relaxation and concentration. Yoga practice is based on eight main levels all aimed at helping the individual to remove any disturbance resulting from upsetting psychological and physical stimuli.

Some of these levels imply the use of special breathing techniques to achieve maximum concentration and the final enlightened ecstatic state.

Musicotherapy. It involves the athlete listening to expressly selected musical excerpts with the aim of infusing his mind with a sense of peace and fullness.

The choice of the kind of music one wants to listen to is absolutely personal: some prefer classical music, others modern or rock music and so forth. Musicotherapy is often combined with relaxation exercises and even with hypnosis in some cases.

Analytical psychotherapeutic procedures. Psychoanalysis is undoubtedly the best known among these special techniques whose typical approach emphasizes the breaking down of phenomena into their component parts. Many different verbal psychotherapeutic techniques originated from classical psychoanalysis.

Adler, Freud, Jung and other distinguished researchers and psychoanalysts studied and refined some special techniques which, through a very close therapist-patient relationship, help the individual to analyze - and even repress, in some cases - the original causes of his psychopathological symptoms and disorders.

Analytical psychotherapies are especially aimed at identifying the underlying causes of pain and suffering. Treatment takes place through a series of personal interviews having either information gathering or therapeutic purposes to provide insight into the nature of the factors discussed. The number of therapeutic sessions per week generally varies from two to three according to the specific theoretical approach, while standard psychoanalysis normally involves four sessions per week.

Hypnosis. Hypnosis is a psychotherapeutic technique which allows the hypnotized person to modify his approach to the various sources of stress and therefore overcome anxiety. It transports the subject into a separate 'state of mind', thus favoring psychological peace and relaxation while also enhancing the individual's capacity to dream and fantasize.

In the so-called hypnotic state, anxiety-inducing problems and situations are generally perceived in a completely different manner. Consequently, the subject is induced to react in a different way - that is positively - to any anxiety-producing and stressing stimulus.

Other alternative relaxation techniques. There are some other psychotherapeutic techniques - maybe less known but often as effective as the previous ones - which help to reach a condition of ideal physical and psychological relaxation. *They include:*

Vogt's method: it helps to reach total muscular relaxation. The subject completely focuses his attention on all the various muscle groups of his body and gradually becomes aware that they can be voluntarily contracted or relaxed alternatively.

Adjiuriaguerra's method: this technique is also based on the assumption that muscles can be either contracted or relaxed by acting directly on one's muscle tone or emotional tension.

Maltz's method: this relaxation technique is essentially based on personal imagination and fantasy.

Silva's method: it basically helps to stimulate memory, intuition, activity and vitality.

Mental training

Mental training should be defined as a combination of special techniques and instruments aimed at helping the athlete to reach the best psychological condition to handle the competition. We have intentionally referred to mental training as 'a combination of special techniques and instruments' because it is important to underline that there are several methods and possibilities to work on and treat psychological disorders today.

In general, the most commonly used techniques in mental training programs include: relaxation, mental images and music.

Psychological training should be exactly like a suit that is made to measure for every single athlete. The tailor is the psychologist in this case and his ability lies in his understanding of which are the most suitable instruments and methods for each player in direct relation to his personality and all the problems that may arise during the competition and his motivation to personally engage in psychological activities.

Relaxation. This is the starting point in any form of mental training. It allows the athlete to learn how to remove and relieve tension and anxiety disorders, which often cause lapses in concentration and inevitably affect and impair the athlete's performance. Athletes can easily be taught how to relax through the various alternative techniques which were discussed in the previous paragraphs. The most commonly known and used among them is certainly Schulz's autogenic training and all those techniques which directly originate from the standard therapy.

Other widely used psychotherapeutic methods include Jacobson's progressive relaxation technique, biofeedback therapy and, in some cases, yoga and musicotherapy. All these instruments can be used as helpful supports to finally plan a highly personalized, 'made-to-measure' relaxation program.

Special muscle relaxation techniques are aimed at helping the athlete to gradually become aware of the tension in his muscles and also understand and identify the body areas where such tension specifically develops: forehead, neck, shoulders, legs and so forth.

Secondly, they help the athlete to learn how to relax particularly strained muscle groups to relieve tension.

Finally, they enhance the athlete's awareness and ability to stimulate a sense of general physical and psychological well-being throughout his body, while also helping him to learn how to control his breathing and heart rate.

Methods like autogenic training and Jacobson's relaxation technique include a wide range of special exercises which help the athlete to learn and train the ability to distinguish between muscle contraction and relaxation and the capacity to stimulate a sense of heaviness, heat and cold in some specific parts of the body.

Mental images. Imagination is a sensorial activity not activated by external stimuli. It can involve any of the five senses of the human body.

Every human being prepares to handle all the various situations normally occurring in life by creating particular behavior models in his mind. This form of thinking often implies the use of particular images; consequently, imagination becomes a real crucial test, a sort of rehearsal that anticipates the moment when one has to face the real game and is therefore a helpful way for the individual to get ready for the match. Frequently, we are not aware that these important psychological mechanisms are an integrating part of our mental reality. Both tests and experiences inevitably make us understand that imagination plays a key role in the process of improving both the physical and psychological skills in any athlete.

It is obvious that mental images are not utterly sterile, but are produced in relation to one's personal psychological condition. For instance, if a person feels depressed and unsure, he is much more likely to create pessimistic mental images and, in a soccer situation specifically, his imagination is more likely to produce something negative. Consequently, the difficulties of the match will be further magnified, the psychological and physical condition dramatically impaired and the athlete will certainly be overcome with fear and doubts.

Special mental training programs should also be aimed at enhancing the desire to stimulate flourishing and highly positive imagination, that is constructive mental images which can help the athlete to prepare to face the competition in a condition of total confidence and optimism. The athlete's imagination should also be trained constantly by means of a series of exercises which prepare him to form a mental image of himself through fruitful visualization. This is also possible by internalizing the so-called specific personal intention formulae (for instance: "I do not lose heart if I feel my heart is beating very rapidly because this is the symptom that my body is going to try its best!...").

An athlete who is able to produce positive mental images and create a favorable state of mind and high self-confidence before a competition is definitely more likely to play much better than an athlete whose imagination is generally full of fears and doubts. The proper learning of suitable relaxation techniques is the first step in implementing special mental training programs.

After a few months (including two therapeutical sessions a week) the real work based on mental images finally begins. Highly relaxing images are fundamental for the very first approach (for example: "I imagine I am sunbathing on a tropical beach....palm trees are behind me, while the blue wide expanses of the sea are vanishing in front of me...").

Once the subject is able to produce clear-cut and well detailed mental images, the second phase starts and the athlete gradually begins to visualize himself on the soccer pitch. He will learn how to imagine himself running, kicking the ball, taking a free kick or a penalty and so forth. Moreover, he will also learn to accurately perceive all the various body sensations that are produced during his motor performance.

The contact of his foot to the ground and all the sensations connected to breathing will be the first perceptive aspects every athlete should specifically train to further enhance and gradually reach a total sensibility of perceptions.

Later on, visualized mental images will focus more and more on positive competitive situations. For instance, the athlete will try to imagine and remember a specific moment in his sports career when he was feeling at the top of his physical and psychological condition, in a state of fullness and peace of mind with no doubts, fear or anxiety. When such skills are considerably enhanced, the athlete will be able to use this form of mental training every time he thinks it can help him both at the end of a training session and before the match. There is another significant aspect of mental training based on images that should not be neglected: it concerns the ability to work on, and therefore influence, the athlete's imagination to even correct and adjust some technical errors.

Music. Music is also a very helpful instrument in special psychological training programs for athletes. Recent studies carried out in the USA and in Great Britain have shown that music can be used successfully in specific psychological training. Musicotherapy is generally recommended as an instrument to support mental training and relaxation training in particular.

Classical music - some pieces by Vivaldi and Mozart in particular are highly recommended as background music during relaxation to foster total desensitization and control of tension. Many also use oriental music including the popular gong, a musical instrument that the Chinese consider dramatically useful in spreading and enhancing a sense of peace and relaxation.

As was already pointed out, mental training should be perceived as a made-to-measure suit. Consequently, the piece of music one chooses should also be in tune with one's personal tastes. Mental training is a new opportunity that the athlete is offered to improve from the psychological point of view. In conclusion, we would like to underline that, at the beginning, the athlete should learn how to use such psychotherapeutic techniques with the help and under the guidance of a competent sports psychologist who can choose and suggest what best suits the player's particular personality and situation.

SENIOR SOCCER PLAYERS

There are so many examples of 'longevity' in soccer. There are athletes who achieved great success in their 'old' age, thus contradicting the widespread mentality that only young players are capable of great performances. Many wonder at what age an athlete can be considered 'old', and whether athletes also experience a sort of psychological aging. From the physical point of view there are certainly some particular obvious and irrefutable situations that inevitably condition athletic performance, especially in soccer, where direct body contact - and all the consequent injuries and traumas resulting from it - can gradually affect and impair the athlete's performance in the long term. This is exactly the case in soccer, rugby and all the other contact sports disciplines where athletes over thirty years old who still want to play must cope with the consequences of all the various injuries they have had throughout their careers.

However, people have often generalized too much, blaming nothing but physical problems for the athlete abandoning the world of soccer after the age of thirty. As a matter of fact, if one really wants to analyze the reasons why an athlete decides to give up his soccer career at a certain moment of his life, the analysis should also focus on different themes and elements and especially concentrate on psychological aspects, which definitely play a key role in this context.

At this point, the reader may then wonder: 'Is there a real combination of psychological problems and difficulties which can gradually induce even professional athletes to choose to give up their soccer careers?'. We are firmly convinced that many different psychological factors inevitably combine together and cause the athlete to take such an important decision. As a matter of fact, as a thinking human being, the athlete can slowly modify (that is either increase or reduce) his interest in soccer as time goes by. Such a significant change is directly connected to his personal motivations and should be interpreted in light of his individual needs.

In order to better understand the over-thirty athlete and interpret his choice to either continue playing or give up the sport, it is first necessary to understand what soccer really meant to him in the past and whether and in what aspects his relationship to soccer has gradually changed over time. In order to better assess all the various elements that may influence 'senior' athletes' behaviors and choices, we will focus the attention on both internal factors - which are connected to the personality of the individual - and external factors which especially concern the surrounding environment and interpersonal relationships.

Internal factors. One of the most important factors that may influence and modify the over-thirty player's relationship to soccer is undoubtedly connected to the sphere of personal motivations.

As Maslow clearly pointed out, motivations are the main agent that direct the individual's behavior towards a specific goal and always involve personal needs. Nevertheless, individual requirements and drives can gradually change due to several factors as time goes by: personal growth, final satisfaction, natural changes in one's emotional and affective life and so forth. This is why it is fundamental to focus the attention on the athlete's relation to soccer to understand whether it has gradually changed in time. This means that it is important to discover if the needs that were fully satisfied in the past have now changed to such an extent that the individual can no longer consider soccer as a rewarding and satisfactory motivational point of reference.

Final satisfaction is undoubtedly one of the worst enemies of athletes. Very often, a soccer player who has already experienced great success can no longer find sufficient stimuli and motivation, since he has already achieved his most important goals during the course of his career. Sometimes, a player will have achieved all that he can at a certain level, especially if he has been playing at that level for a number of years, always fighting for the same targets and goals. Such is the case of a thirty-two year old player who has been playing on a championship club for ten years and has won every trophy available at that level. This inevitably brings about a sort of motivational flattening and impairment in the long term.

The story is completely different for those athletes who have played for a long time in lower categories and are suddenly 'catapulted' to a higher level at a certain moment of their lives. This could be the case of a player who has played in the First Division championship for years and is now promoted to the Premier Division with his team at the age of thirty or even more. In this particular case, the so-called motivational question is opposite, since motivational charge is very likely to be so intense in this player that he will easily be playing at top levels throughout the whole soccer season. Economic satisfaction is another key aspect which should not be ignored.

There are athletes who have always considered soccer as a means to gain profits. These kinds of players have been accustomed to making reasonable amounts of money for years and are now financially independent. Consequently, once they have gained success on the field of play as well they no longer consider economic gain as a sufficiently rewarding and stimulating purpose to play on.

When an athlete realizes that he is no longer 'number one' (the best player), it can seriously affect his personality and upset his psychological balance. Consider a player who has been the absolute star in his team for years and his name and skills have gained him great popularity and notoriety. When this status diminishes due to personal physical problems or simple coaching decisions, it is dramatically difficult for him to find the motivation to work and play with the effort and determination he displayed as 'the star'.

It is obvious that those who have been accustomed to playing the role of protagonist for a long time generally find it dramatically difficult to accept that their value and popularity have decreased and that they are inevitably considered as average players. Some players prefer to abandon the game when they are faced with such critical situations mainly because, in this new reality, they can no longer find enough opportunities for personal fulfillment to counterbalance all the sacrifices they have made for physical and psychological training in particular and for their profession in general.

Final personal satisfaction may also encourage the athlete to test himself and his skills in other fields. As a matter of fact, there are athletes who have achieved everything during the course of their soccer careers, and when they finally realize they can no longer get any other rewarding profit and satisfaction from soccer, they promptly turn to other professions and fields of life to be provided with fresh evidence of themselves and their abilities. Some devote themselves to other various activities still connected to soccer (coaching or managing for instance) while others begin to work in diametrically opposed areas. It is as if athletes feel a strong desire to test themselves in something other than direct personal sports performance in order to discover their skills in other areas of life. Unfortunately, this goal is often very difficult to achieve, since each profession involves its own difficulties and players generally have too often experienced only those which are directly peculiar to soccer. This means that it is sometimes almost impossible for them to handle other situations successfully.

External factors. The external environment also plays a role of crucial importance in the way an athlete over thirty typically characterizes himself at a psychological level. When a soccer player reaches the age of thirty or more, he often gets discouraging messages from the outside. Journalists may ask him: "How long are you going to play on?" and other questions of this kind. The athlete's performance is increasingly assessed in a different way compared to when he was about twenty years old.

The press no longer concentrates on technical hypotheses to justify a not so brilliant and disappointing performance, but increasingly blames the athlete's personal failure on his increasing age. The athlete - especially if he has a very weak personality - gradually grows convinced that he is now old and that his performance is and will no longer be up to the task and to his original skills.

An obsolete mentality is still deep-rooted in soccer according to which players over thirty are thought to have very little to offer in the match. In reality, this is nothing but mere speculation, since highly motivated players who do not suffer from any particular physical disorders can still give a great deal to the soccer match where personal experience is key and the possibility of constantly learning something new does not vanish at the age of twenty.

The family can also influence the athlete's decision to play on or give it up completely in some cases. The family of a professional player should obviously develop great adaptation capacities to successfully handle all those difficulties that the role of a professional athlete implicitly involves. The athlete's wife and children should be willing to live in a reality that is completely different - both in the positive and in the negative sense - from most families.

Soccer players frequently change clubs and are consequently forced to move to another town. This inevitably causes them to constantly change the reality of their social relations. Players are frequently obliged to abandon their friends to develop new relationships. Their children have to adapt to study in a different school and this can bring about serious problems. In the long term, this unstable situation that is characterized by constant changes may considerably boost the athlete's dissatisfaction so that this may also favor - and even anticipate, in some cases - his final decision to hang up his boots once and for all.

Certainly, the role of the team-group is also very important. If the athlete plays a role of significant importance that makes him feel an integrating part in the team, it can obviously help him to resolve to continue playing soccer for a while. On the other hand, there are also very common situations where a soccer player at the end of his career cannot strike up friendships with the members of his team, especially if it is made up of much younger players.

I would also like to underline that the player's relationship to his coach is key in this particular situation, since the coach should constantly enhance the personal motivation of this type of player while also trying to make him feel particularly helpful for the whole team, even and especially in those situations when he is forced to exclude that player from the team.

Stress is another key factor which may induce the athlete to give up playing soccer. Professional players, who have been the center of attention for a long time and have always acted as protagonists in their private lives too, are often subjected to a great deal of stress not only on the field of play but in their day to day lives. Inevitably, at some point this stress begins to wear on them and they begin to covet a life away from the pressures of the spotlight.

Another crucial aspect that often encourages and supports soccer players' decision to hang up their boots once and for all is undoubtedly the unstable psychological condition that is typically brought about by physical injuries and traumas. When a player over thirty seriously injures himself (a bad fracture of the leg or pulled ligaments, for instance), it may often induce the player to resolve to end his career. The problem is not mainly connected to the seriousness of his injury; rather, the real problem results from the fact that the athlete is no longer psychologically willing to accept and handle the rehabilitation experience.

Traumas and injuries that require excessively long rehabilitation periods can sometimes create psychological depression in the player, who therefore prefers to give it up completely rather than wait a very long time, possibly as much as a year, before going back to the playing field. The player never knows for certain whether he will recover his original efficiency completely and therefore re-gain his position in the team.

When an athlete finally decides to abandon playing soccer, usually many different reasons and factors combine together to produce and encourage the decision. Consequently, it is dramatically important for those who really want to understand to consider the whole psychological reality and condition that a 'senior' athlete is living in the final period of his career.

Superstition

Many soccer players are superstitious. Each time they enter the playing field, they must consider the possibility of having an accident and getting injured.

Good luck also plays a significant role in soccer. Such frequent events as a bad rebound of the ball or a sudden slip may significantly affect the score of the match completely and affect the player's performance and career as well. Possible injuries, unluckily played balls, common fortuitous events and movements and so forth are all integral parts of the thoughts of an athlete who is going to enter the playing field to play a match. The player is perfectly aware that his skills, talent, athletic conditioning and tactical strategy are not often enough to unconditionally defend him against such impending risks. When faced with such odds, players usually look for personal security and self-confidence in practices that go beyond the rational reality and belong to the world of 'the supernatural', applying to those practices that are commonly thought to have a sort of 'magic power'.

What is superstition in reality? The origins of superstition date back to a very distant past. In the age of the Romans, stumbling while crossing the threshold of one's house was supposed to be a foreboding of impending misfortune. Going back in time, tradition testifies everywhere that human beings have always applied to special objects, rituals and practices to gain the favor of both Gods and good luck.

The human being has always dreamt of maintaining control of the surrounding reality to avoid any obstacle which would prevent him from achieving his final goals. Nevertheless, the individual's awareness that some natural forces really exist which cannot be controlled at all (like nature itself, for instance) makes him feel particularly weak, fragile, powerless and even anguished in some cases. In order to defend against such undesirable sensations, players often apply to magical thinking (that is the belief that thinking is equated with doing which typically develops in children), thus attributing to special articles of clothing or jewelry and behaviors or rituals the power and the capacity to protect him against misfortune. This typical behavior becomes increasingly frequent and intense every time the player is faced with particular situations that he considers impossible to overcome and control by means of only his own strengths and skills.

Superstition is common not only in soccer but in all of sport. Not only athletes, but also many coaches, managers and supporters behave in a typically superstitious manner, especially in the period immediately preceding the match.

According to Desmond Morris, the period immediately before the soccer match is usually the most intense as far as practices and rituals against bad luck are concerned. If we examine at random about one hundred common movements and gestures against misfortune that are considerably widespread in the world of soccer we can quickly realize that 40% of them are typically carried out in the dressing room immediately before the event, when psychological tension rises to maximum levels. Players also undertake peculiar practices and rituals while walking in the corridor towards the playing field or directly onto the field in some cases.

In many cases, players already feel a strong need on to be reassured and protected against misfortune by means of superstitious behaviors on the eve of the match. Some coaches prefer to always gather the team in the same hotels for the pre-match meal, others even expect the menu to always be the same before each match, especially when that particular menu can be associated with a past win.

There are some players who never shave their beard before the match, some who generally apply to specific rituals in the way they get dressed in the dressing room, and still others who must enter the playing field last. In short, there is a wide range of peculiar habits that are especially aimed at personally reassuring the player.

Superstitious behavior in soccer can be a positive ritual, especially for those athletes who feel the hypothesis of being defeated as something truly traumatic. Every single player has his own peculiar pre-match behavior, which is practically aimed at creating an ideal state of activation of both the mind and the body, to get the greatest profit possible and therefore boost the performance.

On the basis of his own personality and experience, every single player creates his own pre-match routine that is characterized by special reassuring gestures, movements and thoughts. This 'ritualized' period of time must always be the same and always include the same thoughts, gestures and behaviors to favor total concentration.

All the various practices and rituals that are somehow connected to the period when athletes get dressed in the dressing room are the most common. *Some of them are quite simple:* putting on the left sock before the right one or putting the right shoe on before the left one and vice-versa, lacing up one's shoes twice or even three times and so forth. Others prefer to lower their socks to their ankles during the match. Bobby Moore - captain of the English team and former world champion - was very superstitious and his rituals against misfortune were said to include particularly odd gestures: for instance, he always wanted to be the last player in his team to wear shorts in the dressing room.

Cesare Musatti, one of the greatest psychoanalysts in Italy, used to point out that superstition is one's personal inclination to discover a real meaning in any fortuitous coincidence and therefore create causal connections inside the reality. Superstitious players actually attach their success or failure to the presence, or the absence, of an object or a ritual that has no rational meaning in reality, but which they emotionally associate with success and winning. When a player associates an important win with a particular object (a pair of shoes for instance) in his mind, this inevitably causes him to feel a strong need to use that particular object every time he is going to play a match. In this way, a very simple and common accidental event becomes a real mascot or amulet for highly superstitious players.

The athlete's behavior inevitably reflects his character, and the way he can handle the match is a direct consequence of his personality. The player's personal performance during the course of a match can provide useful information on his skills both as an individual and as an athlete - this is especially true when the player has a weak and fragile personality. At this point, typically unsure and fearful athletes whose self-confidence is very poor, generally attach to external pretexts to find the power and strength they lack in reality; consequently, when faced with negative or unsuccessful situations, they may even find an alibi for this without seriously suffering at a personal level.

Superstition is a clear example of a precarious condition and fragile personality, since it distinctly proves that players lack confidence in their own skills. Superstitious athletes practically admit - without really being aware of it, in most cases - they have no sufficient personal abilities and resources to finally achieve the goals they have set for themselves.

In the psychological sphere of a soccer player, what is really important is the fact that superstitious athletes do behave in a special way (that is, adopt well-defined behaviors) to enter the playing field in a condition of complete serenity and peace of mind, while also being conscious they have done everything possible to play well. It is therefore fundamental for superstitious athletes to be somehow reassured and gain approval. Nevertheless, this does not mean that there is some supernatural or mystical connection between the performance of special rituals and the final score on the playing field.

The fact that everything could be true or false has no importance at all for superstitious athletes, since they deeply believe in those rituals against misfortune. Consequently, if somebody dares contradict them, laugh at them or somehow prevent them from practicing such rituals, this would obviously irritate them and make them lose both concentration and self-confidence. In general, special rituals, practices and gestures against misfortune are not harmful to others, but only help to reduce panic and anxiety in the single player.

"Great confidence in one's own skills", once pointed out Desmond Morris, "is often the only element that can distinguish the winners from the losers in a highly balanced competition. This is why superstition and all the various rituals and practices against bad luck will always be popular in highly competitive sports, in the same way as magic practices were widely used in most primitive tribes whose way of life was fraught with risk and danger".

COMMUNICATION

The main problem we face in educating and coaching young players is finding the best way to organize conditioning and technical planning schedules for youth teams. The fine line between coaching and educating has slowly dissolved in the last few years, as people have come to realize that coaching plans specifically designed for young soccer players should focus not only on coaching the player, but on educating the person as well.

Unfortunately, this is not always the case. It is too often proven that the educational aspect in soccer is totally neglected in some situations. We should always remember that those who work in youth soccer should always act according to the principle that for a young player to finally become an elite player of great renown it is first of all necessary to grow as an individual.

A person who is passionately fond of soccer and decides to start coaching youth teams should necessarily be a person of wider culture than a coach who works with adult players - or his cultural training should be somehow different. This is due to the fact that there are definitely more conspicuous and morally important aspects to consider in youth coaching.

These are two completely different kinds of activity and if a coach manages to achieve positive results in one of them, it does not necessarily translate to positive results in the other.

Special training to coach young players

The main motivation that generally encourages an individual to become a coach is the desire to remain and be still involved in the world of soccer when his playing days are over. Many former players make this choice without seriously considering the nature of the job itself. Many look at youth coaching as a stepping stone to coaching adults while others embark on this activity because they truly love working with young players and they simply want to share their passion for soccer with them.

The above mentioned starting motivations can be both valid and well grounded, provided the subject is clearly aware of the moral responsibility that his choice implies. It is first of all fundamental to understand that coaches working in youth soccer cannot absolutely refer to the final number of wins and successful scores in a season as the sole parameter of judgment. It is not proven that those who have achieved great success for five consecutive years in all the various age groups can therefore regard themselves as great and skillful youth coaches. This is a key concept and, unfortunately, it is still very difficult for people to accept in soccer today.

A competent youth coach should set other important goals. First of all, his main purpose should be to help his players consider and live soccer as a positive and exciting experience in their lives. We should all remember that sport can be practiced even after the age of seventy, and all the various benefits resulting from healthy motor activity in adult age are now widely known. Being competent and skillful coaches consequently means helping young players to love soccer (not making them hate it), while also trying to help them live positive educational and formative experiences and as few frustrating situations as possible.

Too ruthless a selection process or a maniacally competitive soccer environment are very likely to discourage young players and can even destroy their self-confidence. Often, in these situations, as time goes by they eventually abandon the sport.

When working with youth players the coach should always be highly motivated and delighted when he finds out that players can openly express their feelings through soccer. It is not important whether the young player has great potential and the skills of a champion or not: what is really important is that he eventually reaches his own potential.

Not everyone is cut out to be a competent and skillful youth team coach. There are some people who have a special bent for working with young players because they have a natural gift for human contact and emotional relationships. Youth players obviously need to learn while playing in an exciting and stimulating psychological atmosphere where the coach becomes a model to emulate. We are firmly convinced that former players who were typically comfortable on the ball can achieve greater advantages and success in coaching young players, since children naturally tend to develop a strong spirit of emulation towards their coach. Seriously dwelling upon one's real motivations should always be a prerequisite in this context. Only in this way can a coach avoid adopting bad or wrong behaviors which may seriously damage the young players with whom he is working.

The coach's relationship to the young players' parents

Those who have been coaching young players for several years are aware that parents and club managers are potential enemies. We can clearly state, without the slightest hesitation, that parents are the first real enemies, since they too often tend - maybe unintentionally - to rock the boat and hinder the coach's job. In many situations, it is dramatically difficult for parents not to feel completely emotionally involved in their children's soccer experience. We are repeatedly faced with absurd situations where parents feel an excessively strong attachment to their children playing soccer. The problem arises from the fact that parents are firmly convinced that their own children are absolutely the best, so they frequently question the coach's choices without really understanding his underlying motivations. Furthermore, parents sometimes even presume to be more competent than the soccer coach himself. This usually occurs when parents are inclined to praise and exaggerate any competitive experience of their children, basically forgetting that this is just one of the several aspects that combine together to characterize the soccer experience as a whole and the educational process in general.

Parents cannot tolerate their children not becoming top-class players and cannot understand that the coachís special choices and behaviors are generally motivated and encouraged by his desire to work for the good of the young players.

How can a coach defend himself against such critical situations? It is obvious that, for a coach to work well and achieve positive results, he needs to cope with such problems and difficulties. He consequently needs to find the most suitable solutions and make appropriate choices so as to gradually make parents his allies instead of bitter enemies. In a modern soccer club, the coach should always dedicate special moments to interpersonal discussion and dialogue with his player's parents during the course of the soccer season.

At the very beginning of the new season, the coach should meet with his players' parents to express and explain his aims and what he is going to do during the course of the year. When addressing the parents, the coach should be highly convincing and make them understand that his coaching plans will be specifically aimed at educating young players in all aspects: physical, psychological and social. If he manages to convince the parents they will probably begin to consider their children's soccer experiences in a completely different light - which means as an opportunity of personal growth and maturation that allows them to freely express their individual potential - without obstinately concentrating on the purely competitive aspect.

Parents are generally very sensitive to these kind of considerations and can often understand and support the situation when special targets of this type are involved. It would also be important for the coach to meet his players' parents in the middle of the season to take stock of the situation at that point of the year. This would help to analyze and assess the general behavior of the players and understand whether there have been particular problems up to that point. Furthermore, it is also fundamental for a coach to consider the school aspect and be seriously interested in his players' school reports and behavior. The player should not approach his school experience as a direct antagonist to soccer: this principle is of vital importance in the context of youth coaching. Consequently, parents should avoid preventing their children from playing soccer or joining the team for a while as a punishment for poor school progress.

It is fundamental to understand that learning is also possible while playing soccer, that motor activity is also culture and, above all, that motor activity is highly beneficial since it can directly enhance learning at school. Consequently, it is obvious that a coach should always work to find points in common about these critical subjects to discuss and share them with his players' parents. If the player is making no progress or is poorly motivated at school, both his parents and the coach may decide to let him train during the week and exclude him from the regular line-up in the league match. In this way, the player is not kept apart from the group but is encouraged to understand that school also requires utter involvement on his part and can not be taken lightly. Finally, the coach should meet with his players' parents at the end of the soccer season to weigh the general situation and plan new strategies for the next season.

There is a very useful method that can help the coach to improve his relationship with parents. In practice, the coach should draw up a personal report for every single player and regularly record all the various aspects concerning the player's approach and relationship to soccer and constantly keep them under control. You will find a clear example of this on page 64. This special table can include the various phases of the learning process of the player, his learning levels, as well as his relationship to both the group and the coach and may also act as a proof of the coach's competence and professionalism.

This personal report should obviously be brought up to date periodically and should also accompany the player in his soccer path: all the various experiences, levels and categories he will pass through. It will help the next coaches to better know and understand the player with whom they will be confronted. When parents ask the coach for further explanations about their children's possible exclusions or changes of position, the coach should always avoid technical or tactical explanations, but should specifically focus the attention on purely educational elements concerning the player's maturation and final involvement in the group.

The relationship with other coaches

The way a coach handles his relationship with other coaches is also a key factor. In particular, every coach should try to develop positive and friendly relationships with the other coaches working in the club. It is important to understand that the more the soccer club can achieve the goals they have set, the more every single coach will benefit, especially in terms of personal image. Unfortunately, bitter competition and conflicts frequently develop between the coaches of the different teams in the same club. Personal envy and a deep feeling of insecurity are very likely to influence interpersonal relationships which, on the contrary, should aim at friendly and mutual cooperation.

Discussions with fellow coaches is of critical importance, since it inevitably enhances one's professionalism. For a coach to develop a positive relationship with other coaches, he should first of all avoid feeling over-confident and believing he holds the ultimate truth about proper coaching methods. Speaking ill of other coaches and putting them in a bad light is absolutely useless, since evil words sooner or later act as a boomerang that perilously returns to hit the 'thrower'. Young coaches in particular should not make the mistake of thinking they are more competent than their 'senior' and more experienced colleagues.

They may be more in tune on the cultural level, but those who have been coaching for twenty or even thirty years must certainly have plenty of tested ideas. It is advisable for a coach to constantly look for mutual discussion and dialogue. Moreover, it is fundamental for the coach to avoid withdrawing into himself and thinking that the other coaches are nothing but enemies to whom he cannot unveil his secrets. All these problems should completely disappear in a modern soccer club. Furthermore, there should also be constant discussions between the coaches of the different teams in the same club, so that they can openly discuss and share their personal experiences and maybe lay the foundations for further cultural investigation. In particular, mutual communication should be significantly intense, especially when young players shift from an age group or one team to another and therefore change their coach. The personal report could be a very useful support for the coach who is inheriting a new team.

PLAYER'S PERSONAL REPORT

Year........................... Season.............................
Full name..
Date of birth...........................School/Club..
Month of the scouting report...

Overall judgment on the player's performance
Facility for learning	0 1 2 3 4 5 6 7 8 9 10
Attention	0 1 2 3 4 5 6 7 8 9 10
Diligence	0 1 2 3 4 5 6 7 8 9 10
Fickleness	0 1 2 3 4 5 6 7 8 9 10

Motivations
Punctuality	0 1 2 3 4 5 6 7 8 9 10
Absences	0 1 2 3 4 5 6 7 8 9 10
Complaints	0 1 2 3 4 5 6 7 8 9 10

Attitude towards the team
Disposition to mutual communication	0 1 2 3 4 5 6 7 8 9 10
Disputes and conflicts	0 1 2 3 4 5 6 7 8 9 10
Loved by his teammates	0 1 2 3 4 5 6 7 8 9 10
Despotic	0 1 2 3 4 5 6 7 8 9 10

Attitude towards the coach
Respectful	0 1 2 3 4 5 6 7 8 9 10
Can take criticism	0 1 2 3 4 5 6 7 8 9 10
Confident (confides in the coach)	0 1 2 3 4 5 6 7 8 9 10

General behavior in competitions
Anxious	0 1 2 3 4 5 6 7 8 9 10
Fear of the opposition	0 1 2 3 4 5 6 7 8 9 10
Performance	0 1 2 3 4 5 6 7 8 9 10
Individualism	0 1 2 3 4 5 6 7 8 9 10
Can encourage his teammates	0 1 2 3 4 5 6 7 8 9 10

Attitude towards the referee
Can accept his decisions	0 1 2 3 4 5 6 7 8 9 10
Faults	0 1 2 3 4 5 6 7 8 9 10
Yellow cards	0 1 2 3 4 5 6 7 8 9 10
Red cards	0 1 2 3 4 5 6 7 8 9 10

Extra-soccer behavior
Progress at school	0 1 2 3 4 5 6 7 8 9 10
Behavior inside the family	0 1 2 3 4 5 6 7 8 9 10

General evaluation
....
....
....
....

Being afraid of one's fellow coaches is counterproductive: the more a coach fears his colleagues, the more it shows he is terribly insecure and lacks self-confidence. In the same way, the typical attitude of those who believe they are the only competent persons in the club and therefore tend to exclude the others is considerably destructive. There is room for everybody in soccer! Mutual discussion and open dialogue with fellow coaches combined with the ability to carefully listen to their experiences very often enrich one's personality more than any number of pages of literature on the subject. All the mistakes our fellow coaches made in the past may be the same mistakes we will make in the future. We should remember this every time we tend to belittle the importance of interpersonal communication between colleagues.

It is also advisable to promote friendly relationships with coaches working in other clubs. Attending special refresher courses can be particularly useful both for obvious cultural reasons and in order to be constantly acquainted with the various movements occurring in the different clubs as far as new opportunities and jobs are concerned.

Mutual cooperation with the club

For a coach to be able to work honestly and peacefully in a youth soccer club, he should obviously develop friendly and fair relationships with all the club managers. Before accepting the job, he should understand what the club management really expects from him: if they set purely athletic and competitive goals, or encourage fair exploitation and maturation of their human resources, or rather pursue important social and educational objects exclusively. It is practically impossible to think of working in a new club and immediately upsetting their traditional strategy and philosophy. Deciding to accept the new job and their decisions inevitably means sharing their goals. This may sound rather commonplace, but it is fundamental for a coach to realize that the team he is entrusted with does not belong to him. The team is only temporarily assigned to him, he is responsible for his players and great confidence is put in his ability to achieve important social goals.

This does not necessarily mean that the coach should always bow to his club managers and behave as a 'yes man' as people are generally used to saying in America. He should always be able to have quiet discussions with them and fairly express his opinions, provided he does not behave arrogantly. The coach should be aware that he is not responsible for setting the goals of the club. Rather, he should concentrate on the methods and instruments to achieve such goals. A relationship of total confidence with club management is actually based on this key principle and this also explains why the coach should not tolerate any interference from them and any situations of disagreement should be discussed and dealt with at the end of the season.

The coach should also think of dedicating part of his time to recruiting new players. Maintaining good relationships with schools, educators and social associations may help him to spot fresh talent to enroll in his club's youth team. If he succeeds in his search, the club management will obviously be grateful to him. The coach's personal image also plays a role of critical importance in developing a positive relationship with the club. Showing oneself in a positive light, maintaining one's body in a perfect condition and being always receptive and willing to communicate to the external world considerably help to enhance the management's sympathy towards the coach and improves the reliability and the image of the relationship.

The relationship with the players

There will inevitably be personality conflicts between the coach and some individual players. These conflicts can be based on a number of factors, but it is up to the coach to not allow them to disrupt the team. He should avoid favoritism and maintain the same impartial behavior towards everybody and be highly determined to make his players comply with rules in any situation, thus avoiding conditioning his attitudes with personal feelings, emotions and individual preferences.

The coach should always enter the playing field with a clear idea of what he is going to do, while also avoiding communicating his doubts, fears and feelings of insecurity to his players. Coaching should always be his main purpose. This is why he should constantly find new methods that perpetually stimulate learning and seriously respect the individual's motivation to playing. It is fundamental to remember that young players generally go to the playing field mainly because they want to play soccer and anything boring and monotonous inevitably lowers their motivations.

The coach's relationship with every single player should always have a special aim within the context of the group and reproaches should consequently be motivated according to the final goals of the whole team. Serious problems may arise from the coachís relationship with the best player in the group. Skillful and talented players often receive particular messages from the outside that are likely to make them feel somehow 'different' from their teammates. A competent coach should always avoid confirming such critical inputs and information coming from the external environment (supporters, club managers, parents, for instance) in his direct relationship with the player. Skillful players should never be told by their coach that they possess a remarkable talent or play better than their teammates.

Furthermore, their teammates should never be directly told that there is a top-class player in their group, since this will inevitably result in conflicts, jealousies and bitter competition that will certainly impair the spirit of cooperation in the group sooner or later. The most talented player should not be offered special privileges; rather, the coach should take care to prevent him from being unconsciously influenced by all the possible messages coming from the outside. Moreover, if he acts as a 'prima donna', the coach should immediately intervene and speak to him, specifically focusing the attention on his personal need to be constantly appreciated and accepted by the group - a need typical of children in the so-called developmental age. It is fundamental to help him to understand that his acting as a 'superstar' will inevitably stimulate bitter jealousies and feelings of competition on the part of the people around him, so that his relationship with others will become increasingly difficult. The player who has a swollen head because of a sudden success - very often, he cannot be personally blamed for this - should promptly realize that he will be nobody at all without the support of the whole group and that his superior soccer skills will be practically useless.

The coach should always control and balance his ability to repress and reward. In this sense, every young coach should be aware that we all have completely different opinions on the subject and that our own individuality directly results from our personal past experiences. There are people who can restrain their emotions very easily and hardly speak in praise of somebody, while others generally behave in a completely different manner. It is advisable for the coach to understand his weaknesses and try to modify his attitudes as far as possible. An excessively marked disposition to repress one's feelings - as well as an exaggeratedly lax behavior - indirectly suggests feelings of personal insecurity about one's own role and about one's capacity to be a competent coach.

When running special courses for soccer coaches we have often been asked how one should behave to best handle the problem of the team captain. In the reality of soccer the role of the captain typically identifies a player who is responsible for handling the relationships of the team with the referee thanks to his own merits. Undoubtedly, his is a task of critical importance and delicacy that may also have significant implications in the player's personal growth. For this reason, we are firmly convinced that, in youth soccer, the coach should take care to study the best way to allow all of his players to pass through this important experience. Many coaches assign the captain's band to a different player either every match or once a month. Others consider the role of the captain as a way to reward a player who has worked hard during a particular period. The various solutions can all be taken into proper account; what is really important is to make one's choices with regard to the personal maturation of every single player.

Communication

Every human being naturally tends to satisfy his individual needs by adopting special behaviors, many of which are specifically aimed at developing new contacts and relationships with other individuals so as to finally appease his condition of need and personal requirements. All the various methods and means whereby human beings tend to approach their fellow creatures combine together to characterize what is typically defined as **communication process**. Nevertheless, there is another type of communication that naturally concerns every individual: a very important communication process develops inside the human body so as to allow it to work properly.

The nervous system, the endocrine system and the cardiovascular system are all key structures that favor the movement of information through the innumerable cells making up all the various organs and systems in the human body. A muscle can work properly only if there is suitable communication between the muscle itself and the brain and this is possible thanks to the processes occurring in the nervous system. Hormones are important means of communication whose main function is to regulate all the primary needs of our body: hunger, thirst, sleep and sexuality. In short, every human being is characterized by two different communication processes: internal communication, on which both medical science and biology specifically focus the attention, and external communication, which is significant food for thought in the sphere of psychology.

Several anomalies - namely diseases - may impair the internal communication process, while serious pain and suffering may upset external communication.

External communication directly favors the birth and development of interpersonal interaction between human beings and these relationships play a role of critical importance since they help to satisfy one's basic social needs. For the external communication process to develop successfully, the presence of at least one other person is prerequisite. The transmitter first sends a message; the receiver gets the message and decodes its meaning.

It is practically impossible to avoid any form of communication (Watzlawick). For proper communication to be possible, both the sender and the receiver must share a common code, so that the meaning or information contained in the message may be interpreted without error. This obviously means that the receiver must be motivated to understand and possess the right instruments to decode and finally interpret the message. A clear example of this is offered by two persons speaking two different languages: a person who is speaking Chinese cannot be understood by an individual who does not know this kind of linguistic code and cannot therefore decode and interpret the original message. Human beings typically communicate by means of two different external communication processes: verbal and non-verbal communication. Verbal communication is mainly based on words that can be codified in various ways such as writing. Writing is a code; those who cannot read cannot decode written messages.

Verbal communication. This is the form of communication that is typically favored in interpersonal relationships by common social conventions. Overt spoken language is the most widely used form of communication to rationally convey messages. This is undoubtedly the oldest form of social communication whose origin dates back to the distant past, while writing was introduced at a later stage as a means to express thoughts and words. Writing undoubtedly marked a turning point in the cultures where it first appeared, since it helped to codify the needs and the thoughts of the human being. Today, we get to know the past of those important cultures rather well, thanks to the ancient documents and writings that have been handed down to us.

Interpersonal relationships are possible only if both the transmitter and the receiver know the codes of communication (namely, written and spoken language). People generally find it difficult to communicate and confront other individuals when they are unable to properly use such codes. This is the case of a child coming from the South and moving to the North, who is inevitably plunged into a reality using completely different linguistic codes from those he had been unconsciously using until then. This child is generally considered to be poorly gifted - often at school, too - but, in reality, his problem is mainly due to the fact that he hardly knows the codes of communication that are peculiar to the new environment. Linguistic codes very often trigger conflicts between people, although they were created with the aim of favoring mutual communication between individuals. Every reality and environment has its own peculiar code. Every geographical region, every occupational sector, some particular periods in the life of an individual - adolescence, in particular - apply to specific communication codes that create real linguistic groups. In reality, a neophyte joining one of these communities must get acquainted with the use of such special codes before becoming a real integrating member of the group.

Non-verbal communication. This is a general term covering any and all aspects of communication that are expressed without the use of the overt, spoken language. Gestures, body positions, facial expressions, glances, tone of voice and the like all fall within the realm of the components of a communication system that transmits information and conveys messages without the use of what is specifically linguistic.

Non-verbal communication is the oldest and most genuine way for an individual to make himself understood by others. Children apply to this form of communication even before they can speak.

The most significant aspect of the non-verbal communication process is connected to the fact that many individuals often apply to the spoken language as a way to hide or mask their real thoughts. We often say the contrary of what we are really thinking, since we are often encouraged by different motivational situations; for example, we may reward a person by means of words while thinking the very opposite.

Not always is this common behavior the direct consequence of personal instrumental needs or secret schemes. Sometimes, it simply results from the human need to hurt someone else's sensibility. However, non-verbal communication is very difficult to 'mystify'; this is why we often communicate a particular message through our words, while our body, gestures and glances communicate the opposite, which typically corresponds to the naked truth. This obviously bewilders our interlocutor who cannot understand whether he should believe the first (verbal message) or the second (bodily message) piece of information. When working with children - and other people, in general - we should always try to be as logical and consistent as possible when we need to communicate something, because children are definitely more inclined to give greater importance to non-verbal communication.

Non-verbal communication also conveys messages of which we are completely unaware. Consequently, we often communicate particular information to our interlocutors without realizing it. This is why serious situations of mutual misunderstanding may sometimes develop, of which we cannot always understand the real underlying cause.

Non-verbal communication in soccer. Like in all the various fields of our everyday life, non-verbal communication also plays a role of critical importance in the world of soccer. Any soccer experience actually offers us significant hints for further consideration that help us to understand the mood and emotions of the people around us. The body is the key element of the communication process in soccer and all the various messages that the individual wants to convey to the outside reality inevitably pass through it.

In soccer we can easily find a number of situations where non-verbal communication is key. Play itself - team games in particular - is a non-verbal communication mechanism. More concretely, passing the ball to another player is a clear example of non-verbal communication. In soccer - and at the youth level, in particular - passing the ball and both the quality and the frequency of passes are inevitably influenced by the type of interpersonal relationship developing between players. A player is obviously more inclined to make a pass to his teammate with whom he has developed a friendly relationship specifically based on mutual respect and esteem, rather than to a fellow player he has always judged in a negative light both at an affective and technical level.

Bodily contact is another helpful non-verbal element whereby players can communicate messages to their opponents. Non-verbal communication also helps to suggest the player's personal disposition and approach to soccer.

Regularly arriving early or late at training sessions or wasting time while practicing workouts should accurately be analyzed as significant behaviors through which the player may communicate his inner psychological condition and disposition to the soccer experience in that particular moment.

Important cues can also be suggested by the players' behaviors when they are gathered together in the dressing-room before the training session. When positive and friendly relationships develop between players, the players are generally very likely to hang up their clothes near those of their teammates as a sign of mutual attachment. If the coach can accurately observe such apparently trivial but important behaviors, it can help him to understand a lot of things about the situation inside the group. It is fundamental to be able to carefully analyze mutual communication processes in the team's interpersonal relationships and it is also important for a coach to read between the lines of what players are constantly trying to communicate to him. In many cases there are particular situations where the player acts in a certain way to show hostility to his coach, while his non-verbal communication openly conveys a totally opposite disposition.

Table 3
The main principles of communication.

According to Morris and Cornop, the study of the human communication process can be basically divided into three main areas: syntax, semantics and pragmatics.

Syntax focuses the attention on such problems as codification, channels and redundancy.

Semantics specifically studies the meaning that symbols should be attributed before being used as relationship instruments. If both the subjects who are communicating to each other do not attribute the same meaning to the symbols they are using, no relationship or communication can exist between them.

Pragmatics specifically deals with the effects of communication on human behavior. According to professor George, syntax corresponds to mathematical logic, semantics to philosophy and pragmatics to psychology.

One of the main principles of the theory of communication is that it is practically impossible to avoid any form of communication. Human behavior cannot have its own contrary, since a form of non-behavior cannot exist. Consequently, it is impossible not to communicate or convey messages. Every single communication unit is a message, while a number of messages between people combine together to produce mutual interaction. Communication necessarily implies personal involvement and therefore defines an interpersonal relationship. The more an interpersonal relationship is spontaneous, honest and genuine, the more the relationship side will disappear in the background of the communication act. By contrast, if the relationship is based on mutual deceitfulness, great tension typically develops when one wants to define the nature of such a relationship; consequently, communication will be specifically focused on this aspect and little room will be left to convey other messages. This clearly helps us to understand how mutual cooperation between individuals can be deeply rooted only when interpersonal relationships are definitely healthy and friendly. In reality, every single communication unit consists of two different elements: the content and the relationship. The relationship aspect directly characterizes the content, so that the communication process becomes pure meta-communication. Communication theory usually structures a communication system into an ensemble of elements called 'units'. Every single communication unit consists of three main elements: a sender S (or transmitter) that encodes a message M (a combination of symbols) travelling through a channel, and a receiver R that receives and decodes the message:

The transmitter feels a particular need and decides to send a message that he needs to encode by exploiting the experience and knowledge he has gradually acquired.

After being transmitted, the message travels independently of anything else for a while. When the message catches the attention of the receiver it can be accepted and decoded. However, the message may also not arrive (completely or in part) because of possible technical disturbances that are typically defined noises. This problem can be easily overcome through redundancy, which defines a superabundance of signals.

At the end of this process, the receiver can finally decode the message: the mechanism whereby the receiver decodes the message can be complete, partial or totally absent. It is fundamental to underline that the message can be decoded only if both the sender and the receiver share a common code. For the communication unit to develop perfectly, the code should be both conventional and well-defined. In other situations, the reality is somehow different: this is the case of one's mother tongue that is typically defined as a highly particular code, since it undergoes constant transformation.

The greatest distinction between codes inevitably concerns the difference between verbal (spoken and written) and non-verbal code. As to the verbal code, one's mother tongue clearly represents the main communication system, as was already pointed out. Typically technical languages or special languages that are highly peculiar to some particular groups (teenagers, for instance) are generally classified as sub-codes.

As far as non-verbal codes are concerned, particular attention should be focused on iconic codes, characterizing the language of fixed or moving images and pictorial representations. Other non-verbal codes are directly connected to human and animal gestures. The message is not a unique signal, but a combination of contents interlaced together. Different codes often combine together in one single communication unit: words, gestures, facial expressions, and body positions towards one's interlocutor. Press reports and written documents in general also communicate several messages to the reader by means of different codes: letters, type, size, layout, images, position of the article and so forth. The same is true for both television programs and movies. There is another aspect that plays a role of crucial importance in the communication process: great attention should also be focused on feedback, that is the reaction, what the receiver communicates back to the sender. In this particular phase of the communication process, the receiver informs the sender that communication has occurred and also reveals his responses.

Every communication unit can have a real meaning only if it is part of a special context. the context helps to define the terms of reference, the parameters that convey a meaning to any communication process. For instance, sounding the horn at a wedding party has a completely different meaning from sounding it in a situation of danger.

THE COACH

In the last few years considerable progress has been made in the field of science applied to soccer. In particular, scientific research has been offering a significant contribution to the knowledge and further improvement of the soccer player. By contrast, similar efforts have not been made as far as the soccer coach is concerned and there is still a lot to discover and investigate about his role, motivations and psychological competence and capacities.

A coach who works in youth soccer, or in the world of professional soccer, generally plays a determinant role both in achieving success - that is positive scores mainly intended in a purely competitive light - and in the maturation and training of the youth player. Consequently, the coach should obviously be extremely well qualified and competent, as only in this way can he shape and positively influence the players he is working with.

Unfortunately, being a former professional player is still considered to be a good background for a person to become a competent coach. Indeed, the technical department of the Italian Soccer Association still tends to specifically privilege former players from the highest divisions, favoring their enrollment in special courses for first and second category coaches. Special conditions were even set to regulate access to professional courses: for example, putting in a certain number of appearances in the highest division as a prerequisite in some cases.

Such a deep rooted philosophy is firmly based on the principle that for a coach to successfully run a group of professional players, he needs to have passed through similar experiences as a player at the top level.

If we accurately analyze the figure of the soccer coach, we can easily see that having a glorious past as a brilliant player is not always enough to achieve successful results as a coach - specifically in the case of coaches running a group of professional players.

On the contrary, many of today's most successful coaches were mediocre players at best with little or no experience at the top levels. They simply understand the game and possess the appropriate personality to coach players. Notable examples are Helenio Herrera and Arrigo Sacchi among the others.

Former champions frequently tend to consider their past as the only instrument on which they should base their role as coach, thus completely forgetting that a coach has duties and responsibilities which are completely alien to most players. On the other hand, the reality is different for those who have very little to remember about their past experiences as soccer players. In general, these persons are often highly motivated to constantly learn and are therefore much more willing to enhance their technical, tactical and psychological skills and knowledge.

The coach's personality

It is obviously fundamental to consider the assumption that not everyone has the personality to play the role of a soccer coach. As stated above, being a former player is not enough to be able to handle a group of players. The ability to properly perform basic technical movements does not necessarily translate to the ability to coach such movements. In short, for a person to become a competent coach, he needs to have a personality that perfectly suits the job.

What are the main attributes for an individual to become a competent coach? They certainly include several important aspects. The coach should be a clever person and should be particularly skillful at handling interpersonal relations. Self-confidence is another key factor. For a competent coach to openly communicate with his group, he should be confident of his skills, firm with his ideas, but also willing to question and discuss them without being overcome by doubts, panic and feelings of anxiety.

Firm confidence in one's abilities and high self-esteem are two fundamental virtues that considerably enhance broad-mindedness, one of the main attributes which should characterize the personality of a soccer coach.

The more a coach lacks self-confidence, the more he will stick to a strict soccer philosophy, unable to shape and adjust it in relation to the players and all the various particular situations he will be faced with during the course of his soccer experience. Moreover, every coach should consider whether he is more suited to coaching youth players or adults. Those who have a special bent for coaching soccer technique and are specifically inclined to experience interpersonal relations at a highly emotional level are more likely to get personal satisfaction from coaching young players. By contrast, those who have a clearly organizational mentality usually prefer dealing with adults. Their main job is to handle each player as a unique personality while at the same time molding them all into a cohesive team unit. In this context, both team strategy and tactics play a role of critical importance.

Curiosity is also prerequisite for a person to become a competent coach and he should always feel a strong need to learn more. The coach should be particularly curious about what the soccer culture can offer him in general, and should also constantly want to know more about his players. On the other hand, he should wish to openly express his own creativeness in order to regularly add something innovative to his coaching plans and suggestions.

Personal motivations and psychological stress

Soccer players often blame their lackluster performances on a condition of psychological stress and fatigue. However, mental strain is not directly caused by strenuous exercise or excessive workloads in most cases. Very often, a reasonable physical explanation for this state of general fatigue and growing uneasiness is not readily apparent. In these cases, fatigue typically has mainly psychological causes and this is why this particular pathological condition is generally referred to as mental strain.

What is psychological stress in reality? What are the main causes that bring about such a pathological condition? What can a coach do in order to prevent and treat mental strain? Some particular situations will be clearly discussed in the following paragraphs. Sometimes, the processing mechanisms working in our brain must handle such a considerable amount of surplus information that it takes too long a period of time and remarkable efforts - beyond standard limits - to process it all.

When mental strain first appears, significant modifications often occur in the brain's mechanisms and strategies to process information. The player inevitably loses part of his capacity to analyze overall external situations, thus shifting his processing skills towards purely serial analysis and exploration. In practice it becomes increasingly difficult for him to assess external situations and events.

A player suffering from severe fatigue may no longer be able to properly view and assess the tactical situation of the match he is playing as a whole. Another key factor that can result in a condition of early mental strain is the tendency to make inappropriate movements or adopt totally wrong solutions.

It is important to remember that when the processing mechanisms in our brain cannot work effectively, physical fatigue appears due to the fact that working muscle groups are not used properly. Also, hard physical work and excessively strenuous exercise may impair the performance of our cerebral processing system.

In many cases, mental strain does not only appear during the course of a competition: it often becomes a constant component in players' everyday lives, specifically during training sessions. Players find it increasingly difficult to bear training from the psychological point of view, even though exercise is not so strenuous and workloads not so heavy.

We are now going to focus the attention on the main causes that generally bring about this state of psychological stress in players.

Factors connected to one's activity. Apart from the fact that the player's performance is seriously impaired either because too large an amount of information needs to be processed in the brain at the same time or because the player has been concentrating for too long a period of time, mental strain may also develop as a consequence of a too small or repetitive flow of information arriving at the brain. Such a reality typically brings about a psychological condition that is commonly referred to as boredom or weariness.

Mental weariness directly results from the fact that the brain processing system is working at too low a level and this consequently causes an impairment - a significant impairment in some cases - of the player's performance. Nothing can tire someone out more than boredom. Weariness can seriously hinder and impair human behavior much more so than an activity requiring harder psychological, and also physical, effort.

Monotony is another main cause of mental strain. It generally develops when one constantly and almost obsessively repeats the same movement or the same combination of actions and activities. In some particular phases during the conditioning period, players are very likely to plunge into an abnormal mood state that sports psychologists typically define as 'monotony syndrome'. It generally results in a lack of interest in the sports activity one is practicing. If such an abnormal psychological condition lasts for a long period of time, this may even cause the player to abandon soccer if no remedial measures are promptly taken.

Always practicing in the same way and at the same time, always thinking about the same things when one is training may gradually stimulate a sense of psychological saturation in the long term. This clearly suggests that the individual is losing any interest in what he is doing. Consequently, training becomes almost unbearable, the player practically does violence to his overall physical and mood state in order not to miss the conditioning session and constantly thinks of going away or giving up completely while getting dressed for practice.

The player can overcome such a condition of psychological impasse only if he manages to find a way to boost enthusiasm and reflection on his personal motivations, can use and constantly stimulate imagination and, finally, manages to escape from excessively standardized and repetitive routines.

Personality also plays a role of critical importance in the way a player can tolerate and overcome both boredom and monotony. Extroverts generally find it more difficult to 'endure' and handle repetitive and monotonous situations than introverts. In fact, extroverts are typically thirsting for new stimuli; this is why they usually get highly frustrated when they cannot find fresh motivation.

Psychological factors. Such factors as individual psychological approach to soccer, personal motivation and will all play a role of crucial importance in the analysis of the problems and situations that can cause mental strain.

Anxiety disorders, feelings of insecurity, and little confidence in one's ability to achieve set goals may result in a condition of psychological stress in many cases.

Personal motivation. When a player is longing to achieve particular goals, it unconsciously results in a special psychological condition that considerably stimulates the player's emotional involvement in training. His strong need to constantly improve and achieve successful results inevitably helps him to work hard and therefore avoid the unpleasant sense of personal discontent which typically brings about weariness and monotony.

The more the player feels a strong need to reach positive results and important goals, the more his approach to soccer will benefit. Mental strain very often appears when the player is passing through a difficult period and his passion for soccer is gradually decreasing. Significant changes in the player's emotional life - which may also be caused by particular situations or events outside the world of soccer - may sometimes affect his personal motivation, so that trying his best on the playing field is no longer a chief goal in his mind.

Problems at school as well as significant modifications in his emotional and affective relations may cause the player to partially shift his psychological energy from soccer to another aspect of his life. In most cases, the individual is not even aware that his indolent behavior when he has to practice and his unusual state of apathy when training are the direct consequences of some important changes in his life outside of soccer. A player is inclined to think that a new job or a difficult and uncertain affective relationship cannot impair his psychological disposition to training. He cannot understand, feels rather doubtful, asks himself thousands of questions, plunges into a state of psychological crisis because he cannot get out of such a situation, when the answer to his troubles is really simple: 'He has something different in mind!...'.

These critical periods are only transitory in most cases and players can soon find fresh motivation and renewed interest in their soccer activity once they have solved their problems. In other particular situations, they find it much more difficult and it takes a longer period of time for them to defeat psychological stress.

Anxiety disorders. Mental strain in many cases is brought about by common anxiety disorders. Anxiety is a vague, unpleasant emotional state with qualities of apprehension, dread, distress and uneasiness that generally tends to affect the individual in all the various performances and aspects of his life. Anxious players are typically afraid of something. In soccer, anxiety is directly connected to the fear of not being able to achieve much longed-for targets. Anxiety disorders significantly upset the individual's normal cerebral activity and inevitably bring about important changes in the individual's approach to the external world.

When a player is suffering from anxiety disorders, he often finds it difficult to rationally assess all the various stimuli coming both from the inside and the outside. These players usually fear they are not sufficiently trained even though they are. They firmly believe their opponents are much stronger and have no weaknesses. The sensations they get from their bodies are frequently considered in a negative light.

Anxious players are extremely careful and alert, their attention levels are so high that their brain processing mechanisms are inevitably overloaded with too large an amount of information in a very short period of time. This obviously tires the brain out since the cerebral processing system must handle both routine activity and such an excess of sudden activation at the same time. Consequently, anxiety promptly changes into fatigue and mental strain. This may occasionally have serious consequences on the individual's health.

Low self-confidence and lack of hope. Anther key factor that considerably helps the player to develop a positive psychological attitude and approach to soccer is directly connected to the individualís self-confidence and hope that he can finally achieve much longed-for goals. When a player begins to think that it is practically impossible for him to reach what he would like to get from soccer, his personal motivations inevitably tend to decrease.

If the player feels unable or thinks he is not skillful enough to achieve certain goals, it can significantly lower his motivation to practice while psychological stress begins to appear unconsciously. Weariness of mind directly results from the player's lack of confidence in his own skills and possibilities. This is sometimes the case with older players who experience severe injuries. They often fear they will not recover their original physical condition and become convinced that their soccer lives are over. This is obviously not a situation which fosters motivation.

Repeated or prolonged failures may also combine to favor a clearly negative psychological condition and this sometimes even causes the player to develop feelings of hostility towards soccer. At this point, anxiety and stress-related disorders appear so that the slightest sense of fatigue immediately becomes nearly unbearable.

Suggestions to avoid mental strain. When dealing with such a critical psychological condition both the tired out player and his coach should investigate the level of personal motivations. They should understand whether or not the player's personal motivations and desires have become weaker and identify the causes if they have.

Careful consideration should also include an accurate investigation into the goals the player has set. It helps to be able to recognize if those goals are practically unrealistic and out of all proportion based on the player's ability level or commitment to that point. Reasonable reflection - as well as proper re-evaluation and slight adjustments to one's plans and ambitions, in some cases - may bring about positive and successful results.

If the coach understands that psychological stress results from a general state of mental weariness and monotony, he should immediately use his imagination and creativeness to modify his coaching method and make suitable adjustments to his conditioning plans so as to make training less monotonous and repetitive.

By contrast, when mental fatigue appears as a consequence of typical anxiety-producing events or situations, special muscular relaxation techniques are generally recommended, since they can considerably help to keep anxiety syndrome under control. When running a team of players the coach should also be able and personally inclined to use suitable methods and instruments to enhance his players' personal motivations.

As a matter of fact, we have already pointed out that 'personal motivation' is an aspect of critical importance, since it often influences the player's performance. Consequently, the coach should also be perfectly familiar with such strictly personal elements of the individual's life so as to best handle the situation.

In the past these problems were often underestimated. Coaches approached the motivational question in two different ways. The first approach - commonly defined 'the donkey's approach' - is based on the assumption that players are all alike and the only effective method to successfully motivate them would be a carrot-and-stick approach, that is applying to both the hope of reward and the threat of punishment as a means of making them try harder. On the other hand, other coaches consider motivation as a real gift that the coach himself offers to his players. This method is known as 'the stork's approach', since it compares motivation to the burden that storks are supposed to commit to the care of mothers, according to the folk legend.

Neither the former nor the latter approach can be considered acceptable because they both deny the basic assumption that motivation originates from the individual himself and is a direct consequence of the player's personality.

Every single player should be accurately 'studied', known and understood by his coach, who should carefully comprehend the real meaning of the individual's soccer experience and consequently offer suitable solutions to enhance each player's personal motivation. Obviously, the coach should be able to apply to special individual strategies to best motivate his players. For this to be possible he should avoid thinking that the members of the same group all share the same motivation.

Only when a coach finally manages to understand his players' personal motivations can he choose and plan the strategy he will use.

Direct methods. Direct methods to motivate players include: personal consent, identification and internalization.

Personal consent. This method applies to the use of both punishment and reward. For instance, the coach can tell his players before the competition. "If you win the match, I will grant you a day off tomorrow". However, this method is not generally recommended for every player. In fact, those who have a very strong personality will almost certainly reject this kind of strategy. This method does, however, suit players whose self-confidence and esteem are generally low. In the long run, this approach cannot help the player to enhance his sense of responsibility and mature independently.

Identification. If a coach manages to develop friendly relations with his players and is aware that they have grown fond and think highly of him, it can considerably enhance his chances at successfully motivating them. The coach can specifically appeal to his relationship with his players in order to constantly motivate and encourage them. For instance, he could convey special messages like: "If you want to work for the good of the team, you must work doubly hard for me."

Internalization. This is the method that clearly focuses the attention on the player as an individual more than any other. It specifically appeals to his personality, values, self-confidence and pride. In this case, the coach bases his strategies neither on punishment and reward nor on his personal relationship with his players, but on direct mutual communication on all the various individual aspects of motivation. Before entering the playing field he may tell one of his players: 'You worked hard in practice, I'm sure you will play a wonderful match'.

Indirect methods. Indirect methods specifically work on personal motivation by trying to modify the environmental situation.

While speaking of psychological stress in the paragraphs above we have clearly pointed out that both monotony and ennui can have dramatically negative effects on personal motivation.

The coach should learn how to properly plan training sessions to avoid repetitive solutions. A competent coach should be able to combine different exercises in order to achieve a common goal. If a coach makes the mistake of suggesting repetitive workouts - so that players already know what they are going to do even before entering the playing field - he can seriously undermine players' motivations and therefore cause critical problems. A competent and talented coach - that is a coach who manages to motivate his players - is able to constantly suggest something new to his players every day. Alternative solutions such as suggesting new exercises or small competitions, switching positions and sometimes changing the training field can certainly enhance players' motivations.

Moreover, the coach should focus greater attention on those players who generally play little in official competitions due to any number of reasons. In particular, he should always try to encourage them and make them feel important for the whole team, making them feel useful and part of the group.

The role of the group in soccer

Soccer is first of all a team game. Consequently, it is of critical importance for a coach to find out and be aware of special situations, solutions, rules and factors that combine together to shape, structure and characterize his group. The group typically differs from other communities of people (like a band, a crowd, a class and so forth) since there is little differentiation or distinction of roles.

When it consists of two to twenty members it is generally defined as a narrow group, a category that includes soccer teams. Narrow groups are usually divided into primary and secondary groups.

Primary groups specifically aim at satisfying the emotional and social needs of their members; they can be either 'real groups of fact' - like a family - or 'voluntary groups' - such as soccer associations.

Secondary groups on the other hand generally aim at achieving special goals, thus binding every single member to one specific role. They include: 'compulsory groups' (those imposed regardless of personal will, like military service) and 'contract groups' whose members firmly accept specific rules and laws in order to achieve set targets.

The group of a soccer team typically belongs to the category of voluntary primary groups, but may also have some particular connotations that characterize secondary groups if it is made up of professional players. Schematically, the group can be defined as a dynamic company of individuals gathered together for some special reason, who mutually perceive each other and are more or less interdependent. One of the main aspects which should be given particular attention in the analysis of the 'soccer team' group is the coach's awareness that combining a number of skillful and talented players is not enough for a team to achieve successful scores and significant goals.

A successful team actually results from the individual needs of every single player combining perfectly together so that each player can find personal satisfaction through the group. The group is not a reality that can be taken for granted, but a real target that every single player should strive for while carefully respecting both the times and the phases through which it can reach its full maturation and definite identity.

The inner dynamic of the group. In psychological jargon the expression 'inner dynamic of the group' refers to the fluent and variable combination of mutual interactions and interpersonal relations between the members of a special group and the external social reality. Such dynamic processes include emotional, affective, normative, organizational, social and relational elements.

Mutual interaction. This is a special process whereby two or more persons mutually influence each other, so that the behavior of one acts as a stimulus for the behavior of the other, and vice-versa.

Friendly and constructive mutual interaction between the members of the same community is prerequisite in order to build a solid group. Communication should be rich in messages and new stimuli. Moreover, every single individual should be able and willing to put himself in the shoes of his fellow members so as to consider any situation from a different point of view. Soccer is a team game that obviously involves mutual cooperation. Consequently, each player should work to create the ideal conditions for his teammates to perform their tasks (roles) in a situation of serenity and maximum effectiveness.

When dealing with such critical problems as the mood of the team, a competent and talented coach should understand the nature of all the various interpersonal relations developing within the group. As a matter of fact, personal conflicts often prevent positive and friendly relations, thus bringing about tension and feelings of anxiety and envy. Successful mutual interaction is possible only if everybody shares and accepts special behavior rules and constantly complies with them.

Set rules, commonly shared values and a well-defined group ideology often act as a real 'glue' that joins all the various members of the team together while also consolidating what is typically referred to as 'sense of membership', that is the sense of belonging to a special functioning system or 'whole'.

Attraction and rejection. These are two important affective elements that characterize interpersonal relationship.

Mutual attraction between the members of a team develops out of similarity and is considerably enhanced as the players grow to share common ideals. When attraction is particularly strong, it helps the members of the group to overcome tensions and difficulties that typically cause stress for competition.

Rejection (or repulsion) is a feeling that does not necessarily imply bitter hostility. It generally arises when a person feels utterly different from his peers. In this case, it is difficult to accept others from the cultural and ideological point of view. This can cause feelings of indifference towards meaningful relationships.

Conflict. Conflict is an integrating part of everyday experiences in any soccer group. Individual needs, psychological tension and feelings of anxiety inevitably cause conflicts within the team. Mutual competition often triggers mutual conflicts.

Competing against another player for the same position as a team regular, for a role as a leader in the team or a privileged relationship with the coach may all be potential causes of mutual conflicts within the group. Very often, conflicts also develop as a consequence of 'transfer' situations. In this case, the player transfers and re-experiences the conflict he is experiencing in an external relationship - with his parents, for instance (the father in most cases) - in his relation with one of his teammates. Occasionally, mutual conflicts may also result from the problem of holding and handling power inside the group.

Development. As we have already pointed out in the paragraphs above, the group should be considered as a final goal, and never as a starting point that can be taken for granted.

Each soccer team has its own peculiar characteristics as a group which are also connected to important organizational factors. First of all, it is fundamental to consider that new players are added to a team at the beginning of every season and this obviously influences and modifies the dynamic structure of the existing group. The 'old guard' will inevitably try to defend against newcomers at first, but they are gradually accepted and integrated into the original group as time goes by.

The general plan aimed at leading the group to full maturity, to that critical target defined as 'life in lively activity' ('...We stay together to achieve a common goal'), inevitably passes through the development of some fundamental phases that are often highly problematical.

Phase of the subgroups. This is undoubtedly the most difficult period that a coach must handle. The group is broken into several subgroups that compete and rival each other in bitter conflicts to hold the power and the role of leader inside the group.

A clear example is that of a big political party (the group) that is divided into several rival factions (subgroups) competing for power, thus favoring the interests of the subgroup over those of the original group.

This often occurs in soccer teams, too. The original group may divide for various reasons and result in several subgroups that can be clearly identified because of their distinctive features: the old, the young, the learned, the rich, the regular players, the reserves, those who speak a foreign language or a different dialect and so forth.

Each subgroup is structured as a real group. In reality, this causes vital energy and general interest to be taken away from the original group, since every player is directly involved in the interests of his subgroup, thus depriving the main goal of the group of part of their personal motivations. In order to successfully pass through this critical phase, the coach should help the members of his group to understand the situation and its consequences, trying to enhance and re-direct their personal motivations and interests towards the main goals of the group as a whole.

Serious problems and difficulties may also arise due to excessively long pauses in the soccer season (the winter break, for instance), since the members of the group do not meet and cannot spend time together during this period. Obviously, these objective problems cannot help to overcome such a critical phase.

The scapegoat. When the 'subgroup' phase is finally overcome, the so-called 'scapegoat phase' may begin. The scapegoat typically defines a member of the group to whom the others direct their own aggressiveness.

In this phase, the scapegoat-player is blamed for any negative situation or event occurring within the group. In general, this is one of the weaker members of the team who is inclined to play this role because of his peculiar character and personality which make him the lightning rod of the whole group. When the team loses a match or in case of bitter disputes and conflicts, the scapegoat-player is considered responsible for everything, so that the whole group can defend against any negative situation and avoid taking their own responsibilities.

As a matter of fact, if we can immediately find a scapegoat in any difficult situation and say "he is responsible for what has happened", we can probably forget mutual conflicts for a while, and this may temporarily relieve our discomfort. The group will adopt this defensive behavior and continue to blame a scapegoat-player for the difficult situation until they finally understand that mutual conflict is an integrating part of the life of the group as a whole.

A typically 'defensive' attitude that shares common features with the above-mentioned behavior is clearly represented by the 'leader's attitude'. The leader of the team can be considered the 'lucky brother' of the scapegoat-player. Hate is generally favored in the dynamic mechanism of the 'scapegoat approach', while love characterizes the relations with the leader of the team.

The players' attitude towards their leader is based on full dependence, while counter-dependence definitely characterizes their general behavior towards their scapegoat-teammate. The whole group are involved to select their own leader, who is generally chosen because of his personality, individual skills and abilities to lead the group and communicate something to them. Not always is the leader of the group the best player in the team, since his abilities as a human being must also be of the highest order.

The leader. A competent and skillful coach should know technical and tactical strategies and be able to teach his players appropriate movements and solutions.

The role of the coach should also include special abilities to successfully run and handle a group of individuals; this is why he must be a leader.

Leadership simply means the ability to suggest a special program of work and offer suitable directions, having a definite view of both individual capabilities and final goals. Strong personality and high influence are key if one wants to run a group in a successful manner. For a coach to positively exert his power and influence - that is avoiding pure authoritarianism - he must be first acknowledged by the group. In practice, the coach must first gain the favor and the confidence of his players; only at that moment can the team accept him as a leader.

Many coaches who are appointed to a new team tend to adopt authoritarian attitudes towards their new players. This is a mistake because it is first of all fundamental to make oneself known to the group in order to overcome the physiological sense of mistrust that typically arises when a new relationship develops. If the group as a whole rejects the coach from the start, he can hardly survive with that team for a long period of time, since bitter conflicts and disputes will inevitably develop within the group sooner or later.

The coach's leadership can be characterized by three different kinds of behavior: the authoritarian approach, the democratic attitude and the functional perspective.

The authoritarian leader is he who places himself on a pedestal and personally sets 'the rules of the game' without considering the opinions and points of view of his players at all.

The democratic leader, by contrast, is generally inclined to favor interpersonal relationships and mutual dialogue, always trying to involve the whole group in any situation and decision.

According to this kind of leadership, the group should finally become the real protagonist of the situation and responsible for the team's technical and tactical strategies while passing through a process of gradual but constant maturation. Long experience in soccer clearly teaches us that a leadership combining both autocratic and democratic elements is the ideal solution when running groups of adults.

However, autocratic and democratic elements and attitudes should perfectly combine together for the leadership to work effectively. It is obvious that, in soccer, the coach needs to act in a mainly autocratic manner in some particular cases, specifically when he has to take important decisions in a very short time. This typically happens in some particular situations during the match, when the coach decides to switch marking positions, roles or make substitutions.

As for coaching young players, the most suitable and effective form of leadership is undoubtedly the so-called functional leadership. This particular method for handling a group - specifically involving significant educational goals - tends to favor a power rotation process within the group according to individual skills, tasks and situations. In this way, every single player can directly live the important job of handling a group as an educational experience stimulating personal maturation.

The coaching staff working with youth teams should specifically aim at shaping characters and enhancing players' maturation mainly as individuals. Individual growth should also include the individual's ability to hold power and handle a group so as to avoid shaping completely dependent personalities.

If the style of the leadership is key, we believe that it is still more important for the leader to display empathy. Empathy can be defined as the ability to share another person's feelings and experiences and understand how he feels when faced with a particular situation. Empathetic coaches are able to understand the feelings of the players sitting on the bench and share anxious players' fears. In this way, the relationship between the coach and his players obviously becomes closer, more intense and positive.

Socio-metric techniques. Applying to special socio-metric techniques may be a helpful support for the coach who wants to better know the inner dynamics developing within his group.

The studies and researches that professor Jacob L. Moreno had been carrying out since 1934 finally helped him to plan a purely social-psychological approach to the reality by means of special instruments typically known as 'socio-grams' (in socio-metry, the word socio-gram refers to a diagrammatic representation of the structure of interactions between the members of a group and helps to measure, quantify or formalize social interpersonal relationships). Moreno's techniques primarily consist of laying out the network of interrelationships that exist between the members of the group by means of special socio-metric tests which can be easily used by all those coaches who would like to know something more about the team with which they are working. Each member of the group is given a special questionnaire where he is asked to select which other members of the group he likes or dislikes, would or would not be willing to trust or to work with, spend time with and so forth so that everybody can secretly express his personal opinion about the sympathy, reliability and competence of every single member of the team.

The questionnaire generally includes an important distinction between the questions specifically aimed at identifying the group structure for both general activities and special tasks (socio-group) and the questions that mainly concentrate on the structure of the group from a purely psychological and affective point of view (psycho-group).

In order to better identify a potential socio-group, players could be asked to select which members of the team they prefer to practice with or which teammates they would appoint to take a conclusive penalty kick. By contrast, if the test aims at defining a potential psycho-group, it should include questions concerning the individual's emotional and affective life such as: 'Whom would you share your bedroom with?', 'Which member of the group would you select to sit with at dinner?' and so on.

The subject should be allowed an unlimited number of choices to answer each question, but the number is generally reduced to three different choices for reasons of convenience. Careful analysis of the answers and accurate data processing clearly help to understand the dynamic nature of the relations within the group. Socio-metric tests also help to identify the most popular member in the team, the most loved player, the player that players trust most at the soccer level. Furthermore, they also show if somebody feels isolated or is not integrated in the group or if several subgroups have developed within the team that are in bitter conflict with each other.

Socio-grams may also act as useful supports for the coach, since they can confirm or deny hypotheses or doubts he may have about interpersonal relationships between the members of the group.

Communication. Soccer is undoubtedly one of the sports where communication plays a role of critical importance in light of the final score. Passing the ball is the peculiar form of non-verbal communication that typically characterizes this sport.

When excellent interpersonal relations have developed between players, the quality of play also benefits considerably, since passing (that is communication) is not hindered by negative personal feelings or mutual conflicts. When two players are in conflict with each other, they are very unlikely to frequently pass the ball to each other while on the playing field, and even when they do pass the ball the quality of their technical movements will not be very high. These situations are very common in youth soccer, but emotional and affective relations inevitably play a key role in adult soccer, too.

The coach should learn to communicate honestly if he wants to achieve successful results. Fair and open communication certainly helps to improve interpersonal relations. This is why the coach should first learn to reflect upon the effects that his words might have on his players.

Moreover, the coach should understand that he cannot convince his players simply by raising his voice. First of all, he needs to be highly motivated and firmly convinced of what he is saying, otherwise his doubts and weaknesses clearly appear in the communication process (meta-communication), thus arousing a sense of perturbation in those who are listening. In addition, the coach should be a good listener and be able to analyze the messages he gets in reply to his communication (feedback).

Communication between human beings does not only develop at a verbal level, as was already pointed out in the paragraphs above. Several forms of non-verbal communication also exist that are undoubtedly much more spontaneous and direct. Grimaces, body positions, sighs, gestures and so forth very often communicate more than words. This is why the coach should also learn how to analyze and interpret non-verbal language.

Dealing with non-verbal communication also helps the coach to understand something more about interpersonal relations between his players. Only in this way can he realize if mutual conflicts have developed within the group that are not expressed verbally.

The pre-match camp

Soccer players often complain when they have to leave for the pre-season or pre-match training camp. The pre-match camp has always been a matter of discussion among club coaches, players and journalists and two contrasting theories have developed about the subject. On one side there are those who believe that the pre-match camp plays a key role in the team conditioning process, while others are firmly convinced that it is nothing but a harmful instrument in most cases and should therefore be used as seldom as possible.

As typically happens in most conflicts of opinion, balance is the most reasonable solution. This is why we think it advisable to handle the 'pre-match training camp' question with an open-minded approach, considering both the real benefits that this method can offer to the soccer planning process as a whole and the risks and difficulties that it may bring about.

In practice, three different types of training camps exist in soccer: the pre-season camp, the pre-match camp and, in a very few cases, the post-match camp.

When dealing with the problem of the pre-season or pre-match training camp, it is first of all important to focus the attention on mainly psychological aspects. This means that it is fundamental to carefully analyze how every single player with his own individual personality may react to this kind of experience. We are now going to analyze the most important psychological problems that may arise during the pre-season conditioning period. The pre-season training camp has now become a habit in professional soccer. Every year, professional soccer teams move to peaceful mountain resorts for a certain period of time and try to lay the bases for the whole conditioning process that will develop throughout the soccer season. We are not going to analyze technical and physiological aspects in detail in this context, since we just want to concentrate on purely psychological factors.

The group. The first important factor to consider is connected to the presence of new players introduced to the team for the first time during the pre-season training camp. During this particular period when the whole team is gathered together to live and share common experiences, they should be integrated into the existing group. However, full integration is not so easy and automatic in reality as it is generally thought to be. The group as a whole is a very complex entity in which such factors as mutual competition, attraction and rejection play a role of crucial importance.

The fact that the players belonging to the original group are somehow reluctant to immediately accept the integration of new elements into the team is understandable. They fear that the interpersonal relationships and psychological balance existing within the group may be upset or that the newcomers may undermine the original leadership. This is why new players can sometimes find it very difficult to be integrated into the team. Some players are also afraid that the newcomers may take their positions in the team or simply undermine their popularity. The problem becomes still more complicated when there are strong and firm personalities among the new players, who are therefore more inclined to impose their will on the others.

During this delicate phase of the pre-season training period, the coach should pay particular attention to the type of communication occurring between the members of his group. Moreover, it would also be advisable to plan special moments for group discussion, so as to make possible mutual conflicts come to the surface and consequently face them at the right moment, before competitive duties require a really mature, solid and compact group.

In order to get more useful information about the inner dynamics developing within his group, the coach could also apply to special psychometric techniques and instruments - socio-grams - so as to get a clear insight into the situation.

Psychological motivations. Apart from paying particular attention to interpersonal relationships between players, the coach should also spend part of his free time (and occasions do exist during the pre-season or pre-match training period) personally talking to every single player.

It is of vital importance for the coach to understand what every single player personally expects from the next soccer season. In particular, the coach should understand the player's individual goals and how hard he is willing to work to achieve those targets. Individual feelings of insecurity can often impair the player's self-esteem so that he loses confidence in his abilities. In this case, the coach should help the player to understand his inner conflicts and finally overcome them.

Through direct contact and personal communication with his players the coach can get a clear idea of their individual personalities and consequently adopt different psychological behaviors to approach them so that every single player can express his full potential during the course of the soccer season. A truly competent and talented coach is one who manages to make every single player express his abilities without feeling inhibited in any situation.

Effects on players' personality. When speaking to soccer players, they often reveal that their coaches sometimes approach and treat them as children during the pre-season conditioning period. Actually, many coaches tend to adopt too rigid behaviors towards their players. In particular, they set strict rules regulating any form of dietary transgression, the time when players must go to bed and even their sexual activity.

In practice, the coach-player relationship that the coach himself creates is very similar to the typical adult-child relationship where obedience, submission and paternalism are the underlying components. Players who have not personally reached full maturity easily adapt to this authoritarian pattern, while others firmly reject it, a situation which can obviously result in bitter conflicts. Many coaches forget that they are dealing with professional players who can consciously understand and decide what is right or wrong as to their personal choices. The pre-match or pre-season training camp is an experience that involves strenuous physical and psychological loads in itself, since athletic and technical conditioning obviously requires players to work hard and get seriously involved in what they are doing. Consequently, it would be advisable to reduce other causes of stress to minimum levels, specifically if they are connected to the player's emotional and affective private life.

Leaving their families or, in a certain sense, 'breaking' their affective relations for about two or three weeks certainly implies hardship and sacrifice that not everyone can bear serenely.

By contrast, a competent and modern coach should favor the model adult-to-adult relationship in his approach to players, so as to help every single player to shape his personal identity based on both maturity and professionalism. In reality, only through the adult-to-adult approach can the player understand what he really needs and will certainly avoid any excess because he will understand that he will personally suffer damage for his own mistakes.

On the other hand, if the player is treated as a child, he is likely to act as a child. He is still unlikely to commit excesses, but only for fear of reproach and punishment by the coach. Moreover, a child-like desire to break rules is apt to emerge in these cases.

Ennui. When the pre-match or pre-season training period is too long, it often becomes difficult for players to spend their leisure time after strenuous exercise on the training field. Ennui often characterizes the player's mood during the pre-season training camp.

Soccer players generally spend their free time playing cards or billiards, some read or watch TV, others spend a lot of time calling their partners or agents (the pre-season conditioning period often coincides with the period when most players are dealing with the problem of renewing their contracts).

A profound sense of ennui may be dramatically negative and seriously upset the individual's psychological balance, thus triggering disturbed reactions. Irritability and severe depression may sometimes appear in those pre-match or pre-season camps where ennui - that may result from lack of communication between the members of the group - reaches excessively high levels.

The coach should also choose a place where the team can gather together for the pre-season or pre-match training camp, always taking all the above-mentioned significant aspects into proper account. Many coaches still believe that players can keep full concentration only if they gather in peaceful hermitages where there is nothing else apart from their hotel, the training field and some animals grazing here and there.

However, walking around at night, watching a movie or spending some time at the disco can really help players to better suffer and relieve such severe psychological stress that pre-season conditioning inevitably brings about.

Whatever can help to motivate players and relieve mental strain during the pre-season training period should be considered with great attention. Players should always be active, receptive and willing to learn. A negative mood state characterized by depression, ennui, feelings of despondency, sadness and related symptoms may seriously prevent players from absorbing what their coach is trying to suggest during training sessions.

Coercion and interdiction do not generally work so much with young players, and as for professional players who are thirty years old or even more in some cases.... This would certainly be too much!

Psychological training. In the last few years, the use of special psychological techniques aimed at enhancing players' performances has been spreading out in the world of soccer. If a coach is going to apply to special psychological supports and include them in his coaching programs, the pre-season training period is undoubtedly the best moment for him to carry out and test this new experience.

It is advisable to include a psychologist in the medical staff of a professional club, since this could certainly help to enhance every single player's performance and the whole team would obviously benefit.

We are firmly convinced that, in a modern club, the psychologist should take an active part in selecting new players, since he could immediately understand whether their personalities satisfy the needs of the club. Personal motivations inevitably decrease - specifically at the end of one's sports career - and many clubs often realize they have made a huge economic investment which proves to be a real failure on the playing field.

During the pre-season conditioning period, the psychologist should first of all offer his personal and professional support to the coach so as to help him understand the inner dynamics of the group. Very often, the coach has neither the time nor the competence to accurately observe and analyze all the various interpersonal relationships developing between his players.

Secondly, the psychologist should begin to focus his attention on every single player and specifically deal with those players who suffer from pre-match anxiety disorders.

During this particular period when players practically live together and share common experiences, the psychologist could teach them how to use special muscle relaxation techniques specifically aimed at helping them to control and relieve anxiety disorders and stress-related symptoms (like autogenic training, for instance). Other alternative methods that are aimed at enhancing concentration could be used in this period so that players gradually learn how to use them on their own during the season.

If psychological training is suggested as a method to enhance both individual and team performance, professional players will certainly get involved and seriously apply themselves since they realize they can personally benefit from it.

The relationship with injured players

Injuries in soccer are a factor of critical importance, since they seriously hinder the whole training and coaching planning process. Many coaches constantly say that they find it difficult to plan their activity - athletic conditioning, in particular - due to the increasingly large number of injuries occurring throughout the season. In fact, the physical consequences of the soccer match and frequent muscle injuries seriously affect the work carried out the week following the competition.

The psychological aspect has always been somehow underestimated or completely neglected in the analysis of the problems that injured players must cope with.

In the last few years, significant advances in medical science have helped to considerably reduce the recovery period in some of the most serious and frequent pathologies occurring in sport - like in the case of a surgical operation to remove torn menisci. However, medical advances have probably helped to turn attention away from those individual psychological factors that may play a key role in this critical situation by enhancing the player's capacity to recover full efficiency in a very short time. In order to better analyze the question, it is first of all fundamental to underline that the recovery period may be shorter or longer even in players suffering from the same physical disorders.

There are players (and we specifically refer to players suffering from bone fractures or undergoing surgical operations) who are highly motivated to face rehabilitation and therefore work hard to recover their original efficiency, while others are more inclined to invest little mental psychological energy in rehabilitation and their recovery period. What are the reasons for these two different approaches? It is difficult to give a clear answer. Anyway, it is obvious that every single player's psychological individuality plays a decisive role in the recovery experience.

Players - and human beings in general - typically experience feelings of fear and anxiety when their bodies lose part of their physical efficiency. Physical disability - even if it is only a temporary experience - is very likely to bring about a state of psychological depression, which means a difficult situation that not everyone can handle in the same way. Actually, some manage to react promptly and therefore recover in a short time, while others find it difficult to direct all their psychological energies to the main goal, that is full physical recovery.

Soccer players usually feel and live these problems and difficulties much more intensely than common individuals, since their bodies have helped them to gradually build a world - the world of their sports experience - where they have fulfilled all of their basic and meta needs and expressed their full personal potential (self-actualization). This is why a player needs to have a highly efficient body that is able to express its full potential.

It is fundamental to understand the psychological condition of an injured player who needs to undergo special rehabilitation treatment, particularly if it will last for a long period of time or when the prognosis for full physical recovery is uncertain. Furthermore, it is also useful to try to understand the surrounding environment and reality that may sometimes offer a positive support for the player to successfully pass through such a difficult experience. This is why both individual psychological motivations and environmental factors should be taken into proper account in the analysis of all those psychological problems that are somehow connected to the experience of physical recovery after injury.

Individual motivations. There are players who can transfer their motivations to competition from the match directly onto themselves.

In practice, all the energy they invested in the soccer match is transferred to another kind of competition, that is physical rehabilitation. These players are able to find the right motivations and therefore work hard while performing special rehabilitation workouts, so that the rehabilitation conditioning session is lived as real strenuous exercise. By contrast, other players do not consider the recovery period as directly connected to their sports experience, but are particularly motivated by intense 'narcissistic' needs.

The strong need for full physical efficiency is an integrating part of their own personality, a need that considerably stimulates them to get seriously involved in rehabilitation so as to recover their best physical conditions in the shortest time possible. These players - who also try to satisfy their personal motivations while practicing sport - typically take care of their bodies, since the body has become an object of worship for them. The 'economic' aspect may also be of great importance in some situations. As a matter of fact, money can often act as a real psychological motivation for most professional players, and the fear of impairing one's physical efficiency is frequently connected to the fear of giving up economic profit for a while. Economic motivation can often be particularly strong in those players who suffered serious injuries early in their professional soccer careers.

By contrast, the opposite is true for many players at the end of their careers: they generally abandon sport after experiencing serious injuries, specifically because they cannot find sufficient motivation to face a difficult - and maybe long - rehabilitation experience.

Motivation to 'affiliation' may also develop in players who are practicing to recover their original physical efficiency after injury. Teenage players, in particular, are more inclined to feel a strong need for prompt physical recovery so as to also recover their position within the team-group. The thought of being excluded from the group for a certain period of time due to physical disability obviously arouses a sense of discomfort and discouragement in them and encourages them to invest all of their energies in rehabilitation.

Environmental factors. The 'family' also plays a key role during the recovery period. Its members can positively influence and therefore enhance the player's motivation to full recovery through all the various messages they send to the injured player both consciously and unconsciously. Living in a warm atmosphere, in a condition of total serenity where the player perceives feelings of affection and love by his relatives can certainly help him not to feel alone in that critical experience.

The family should act as a 'container' for the injured player and constantly stimulate his self-confidence. By contrast, those families (and we specifically refer to youth soccer) who have always opposed the sports activity practiced by their children are very likely to play a negative role in this context. When the child has an accident and gets injured, they generally find new arguments to try to persuade him to abandon that sports discipline once and for all. The whole team can also help injured players to pass through the recovery period more serenely. It is very important for those unlucky players to feel the presence of the group around them during the rehabilitation phase.

All those activities and initiatives that may help the player to perceive the interest and sympathy of the group (his team) are highly recommended. Involving him in training sessions in some way, insisting on his presence in the dressing room, asking him to follow the team at away matches and so forth certainly help him not to feel excluded or far from the group and considerably enhance his desire to recover full physical efficiency in a short time.

The coach should also be very close to injured players, constantly talking to them, encouraging them and making them understand that the team needs them. The more they perceive that the coach is emotionally involved and interested in their situation, the more they will work hard to get back to the playing field. The club managers should also be particularly interested in the condition of injured players and directly follow the various phases of their recovery, so as to make them realize that they are not left alone. The relationship with the medical staff taking care of players' rehabilitation should also be taken into proper account.

The injured player should be the protagonist of his rehabilitation therapy. This means that the medical staff should clearly explain the meaning, use and benefits of all the various rehabilitation exercises he has to perform. He should not be the object but the subject of the treatment and should consequently be able to assess even the slightest improvement.

It would be advisable to use this period of 'forced inactivity' to try to enhance some basic aspects of the player's general knowledge, competence and professionalism. During this period of time, the injured player could be taught special muscle relaxation techniques (like auto-genic training and so forth) or special psychological conditioning procedures (mental training). These kinds of initiatives could help the player to live such a critical phase of his life in a less negative manner, while also offering him the opportunity to improve his psychological performance when he resumes playing soccer after the accident.

Hopefully, new methods for special psychological training will be studied in the near future so as to enhance coaches' knowledge on the subject. We are firmly convinced that many aspects need to be further investigated. The coach should first of all learn to better know himself, his fears, personal motivations and inner conflicts. In the future, greater attention should be focused on specific personal training while selecting and recruiting coaches - specifically those who are going to coach young players. It is also desirable to favor mutual confrontation between coaches and therefore arrange frequent meetings and special workshops to discuss particular subjects.

Handling a group successfully, getting familiar with such critical problems as anxiety disorders and personal motivations, being able to apply to such innovative techniques as auto-genic training and mental training should soon become an integrating part of every single coach's cultural background. In the same way, competent coaches should also enhance their knowledge of all those psychological problems that typically characterize players in the developmental age (particular attention should obviously be focused on adolescence).

Obviously, coaches cannot learn all these elements by attending the simple courses that now exist. It is necessary to develop a new model for constant, highly specialized training to which several important figures, both at the institutional and recreational level, may offer their personal contribution. Certainly, the individual's personal motivation to improve his cultural background is key, since only this motivation can make someone hope to be or become a good coach.

A new coach

Why have so many coaches been dismissed in the last few years?

Is it really helpful to change the coach during the course of the soccer season?

The subject has been under discussion for years now and all those working in the world of sport have been searching for grounded arguments to answer these questions. Sooner or later, all those belonging to the soccer 'intelligentsia' have expressed their opinions on the subject, but in spite of this the answers are still very evasive and too sketchy.

Many have given their personal opinions on the question, all aimed at unveiling the truth: a truth that has been rigged with unfair interests in too many cases. On one hand, there are the coaches - who often feel at ease in the role of victim - who typically stick to a corporate philosophy that has always prevented proper investigation into the causes of the coach's dismissal. On the other side, there are the presidents and club managers who simply take note of the fact that the coach is the only element that can be easily changed in soccer when things are wrong.

Dismissing a coach during the course of the soccer season is certainly a failure for the whole club. Those who feel in tune with the widespread modern mentality may disagree, but careful analysis of the problem clearly confirms that choosing to dismiss a coach during the course of the season means that the club acknowledges they have made a mistake.

The coach is selected and recruited by the club according to the final goals they want to achieve, the main characteristics of the team and the coaches available on the market. When a club finally appoints a coach to a particular group of players, this means they have decided to trust that particular person because of his skills, competence and past experiences. The club is responsible for assessing the situation and finally selecting the coach; consequently, they must take full responsibility for the consequences of their choice.

This means that when the club decides to dismiss a coach, they admit that they failed to carefully assess the situation and have chosen the wrong coach. Several reasons can lead the club to decide to dismiss a coach during the course of the soccer season; however, the point is that the dismissal proves they did not properly assess the situation and all the various aspects involved when they finally appointed that coach to that particular job.

Causes. The fear of failing to achieve set goals is certainly one of the main factors that typically cause a coach and his job to be put under discussion.

Lack of successful results is what presidents and club managers generally fear most. When the position of the team in the final rankings does not correspond to what they expected, the ghost of the failure of an entire sports season usually stimulates in the club managers the need to take remedial measures. In these cases, they can no longer assess the situation in a reasonable way, since emotions inevitably get the upper hand over reason.

The need to do something immediately - so as to solve the situation and restore the success of the team - too often leads the club to choose the easiest solution and therefore identify a scapegoat, the coach in most cases. In this way, they clearly forget that for a coach to transfer and communicate his strategies to his players, he obviously needs time. Unfortunately, soccer cannot wait today.

Obviously, the club cannot analyze the situation in total serenity and coherence. In general, they are unlikely to wonder whether the goals they had set at the beginning of the season were unrealistic if compared to the real objective value of the team. In reality, they assume that the new coach will do something better than the one they have dismissed and cannot reflect upon the difficulties that the new coach will inevitably deal with.

Difficult interpersonal relations within the team and the club in general occasionally represent another significant factor that may cause the club to break their relationship with the present coach. Factors could include unfriendly and hostile relationships between the coach and the management, the coach and his players, or the coach and the external world moving around the team (spectators and supporters, the press and so forth).

Misunderstandings, conflicts, dissensions, and superposition of roles may become elements of friction upsetting the relationship between the coach and the management of the club.

When the coach accepts a position, he does not know the reality of the club and the personality of the managers completely in most cases. In some soccer clubs the management have been inclined to interfere in technical choices. Obviously, this is possible only when the coach tolerates these rules. Consequently, when a coach is recruited in a club where the management acts in this way, either he promptly adapts to the situation, or mutual conflicts develop. If the two sides cannot reach a compromise, the coach's dismissal is inevitable. This is why it is fundamental for the coach - and for the club management as well - to carefully assess the situation, including purely relational aspects, before signing the contract.

Serious problems may also arise if the coach wants to play the role of the protagonist within the club. There are presidents who love to get undivided attention and hardly tolerate being put in the shade by a coach who has a strong personality that consequently helps him to attract other people's interest and attention. Hostile relations between the coach and his players may also bring about serious problems.

When the coach cannot gain the favor, confidence and respect of the whole group, when the team is divided into several subgroups, or when players can hardly bear their coach, mutual tensions and conflicts are likely to develop which are generally very difficult to handle. When mutual conflicts and tensions can be expressed verbally or lay dormant for a certain period of time, they inevitably contribute to impair the performance of the whole team. In these cases, the club should act as a mediator; in general, club managers are often more inclined to support the arguments of those who oppose the coach, specifically if the most skillful and talented players in the team take sides with the 'rebels'.

A coach who has just been appointed by the club to lead a new group of players cannot think of imposing his ideas on the group without previously trying to understand if the members of the team share his own ideas.

All the various changes in the play system, in training rhythms and workloads, in positions, roles and duties on the playing field may stimulate bitter conflicts in the players' relationship to the coach. In particular, this generally happens when players realize they cannot get personal benefits (fame, prestige, performance, money) from the new coach's rules and strategies. Changing always involves feelings of anxiety, psychological tension and even fear, in some cases, specifically for those who have been accustomed to a certain way of living.

It generally takes time for players to accept the new coach, the new reality and the new technical and tactical philosophy - specifically for those personalities who are particularly fragile and obviously find it more difficult to change course. In addition, the level of players' personal motivations can considerably influence their approach to the new coach and his new soccer strategy. Those who are highly motivated to constantly improve are usually more likely to accept the new rules than those who already feel completely fulfilled and stick to their conservative positions.

The coach's problems and difficulties may also arise from his personal relations with both supporters and mass-media. Supporters - fan clubs and well-organized groups of supporters, in particular - unfortunately hold great power in modern soccer. In some cases, they even manage to influence the decisions of the club as to particularly important matters.

The coach who cannot gain the favor of these groups of particularly enthusiastic supporters generally runs serious risks. This is why it is not so uncommon to see coaches who tend to focus their attention and throw luster on those enthusiastic admirers of soccer.

The coach should also gain the favor of the press. His public image should be perfectly studied. Mass-media typically holds great power and plays a key role in determining either the success or the failure of a coach.

Reactions of the team. The change of coach during the course of the soccer season very often awakens reactions within the team - in particular, players personally react to the change of the coach as individuals first, rather than as a compact group of players.

Consequently, there are players who will certainly find it more difficult to accept a new coach, particularly when they had developed friendly relationships based on mutual confidence with the outgoing coach and when their interpersonal relations allowed them to fully satisfy individual motivations. These players may even consider the change of coach as a real danger for themselves. The fear of losing their positions in the team or failing to get accustomed to the new training and coaching methods may upset these players so that they have great difficulties in accepting the new coach at the psychological level.

When the whole team is passing through a period of crisis, the structure of the group very often experiences the so-called 'subgroup phase' and it is not so difficult to identify two opposing subgroups developing within the team during this critical period. One subgroup is still very close to the ideas of the former coach and therefore struggles to defend him in public. The members of the other subgroup view the change of coach as a means to improve their personal situation.

The change of the coach obviously upsets the inner balance of the group so that the inner dynamics are put under discussion again. The members of the subgroup that previously held less power are now motivated to play their cards right aiming at finally gaining the leadership in the team. The members of this subgroup are typically more likely to welcome the new coach with great benevolence and immediately offer him their personal support and cooperation.

By contrast, the subgroup that practically 'held power' and played a leading role in the team of the former coach will probably find it more difficult to feel willing to welcome the new coach warmly and will adopt a typically defensive attitude and cold approach to him at the beginning.

This clearly shows that the new coach has a particularly tough and delicate job to perform. First of all, he should carefully assess the situation and act accordingly, trying to reform the cleavage within the team which is the real obstacle that prevents the group from achieving important goals. A team that is split into several subgroups can hardly achieve successful results and important targets, since players inevitably concentrate their energies to make a bid of power rather than to reach purely athletic and competitive goals.

Sometimes, the team makes a successful score in the match that immediately follows the change of the coach. This is not often due to the change in itself, but to the fact that players can overcome the condition of psychological depression that had developed in the previous situation.

The relationship between the former and the new coach

In order to get out of that critical situation, it would be advisable that the outgoing coach and the newly-hired one develop a positive relationship so that they can openly discuss the situation and all the various problems concerning the team. The new coach should be accurately informed about the work that has been carried out: in particular, he should be told everything about his technical and tactical coaching methods and athletic conditioning as well.

We also think it convenient for the new coach to be carefully informed about the inner dynamics and interpersonal relations within the group, about the feelings of both sympathy and rejection or mutual conflicts between players, about the best way to deal with every single player and about each player's individual personality.

This can obviously make the job of the new coach much easier and also helps him avoid the same problems that the former coach had not been able to solve. For this to be possible, the two coaches should overcome mutual conflicts at the professional level and reason and act for the good of the whole team.

Unfortunately, a coach very often leaves his team because he is dismissed by the club. Consequently, his mood state is not kindly disposed to the new coach: he feels highly depressed and frustrated and is not particularly willing to offer helpful information to the newcomer who has taken his job.

PARENTS

A child's experience when approaching sport is too often conditioned by his parent's mentality. Frequently, parents load the child with their own motivations, past frustrations and vanished dreams.

Undoubtedly, those parents who do not want to damage the sports experience of their child and consequently development of his personality, must carefully consider the meaning they personally attribute to sport, their own mentality and the way they intend to live the sports experience of their children.

Parents' approach to soccer

It is important that parents develop a positive relationship with soccer. By positive relationship we mean that they should be aware and accept that soccer is not only a sport, but must also be a school of training for life, a means and not an end, to help young players to grow in psycho-physical harmony. Parents frequently have erroneous concepts of soccer: they wrongly interpret the experience in too hedonistic a light and are too firmly tied to the desire to search for a higher social status, not only for their children, but for themselves as well. The worst thing is that parents are not aware of their attitude. On the other hand, we can also find parents who have a prejudice against soccer and are firmly persuaded that a soccer experience is a waste of time.

There are parents who were never personally educated for soccer and are therefore convinced that soccer is harmful as it may cause injury and violence. Others, as they do not recognize any educational value or purpose in the soccer experience, firmly believe that the energy used for playing soccer distracts from scholastic obligations, thus impairing their child's performance at school.

Very often, these parents prevent their children from playing soccer as soon as they notice a decrease in scholastic profit, and force them to quit their soccer experience without realizing that this will worsen the situation still further, since they do not offer their children the possibility to enhance their learning skills. It is proven that suitable physical exercise also facilitates learning at the school level.

Parents often transfer to their children the ghosts which haunt their own mind: the needs they have never satisfied, their personal failures, the fruits of the education they have received. This happens not only in soccer but also in other situations of everyday life: for example, when it is necessary to make a choice regarding school or one's work activity.

Many people attempt to relive their own sports experience through their children. In this way, they tend to condition their child's way of thinking and create for him special sports models that are totally inadequate for the child's individual reality. These parents are unable to realize that the child's experience is not their own and often end up inflicting psychological violence on the child who can do very little to defend himself in such a critical situation.

A parent must be aware of the risks he may run and the problems that may arise when he does little or nothing at all to understand the emotional state of the child and only desires to make his child live the sports experience as he would like it.

Choosing the child's sport

Sooner or later, the day comes when the discussions relating to the choice of sport that best suits the children begin in most families. It is important to underline that the child's choice of the activity he is going to play should be as spontaneous as possible. Very often, however, it is one of the parents who directs the child in his decision. There are even times when parents do not allow their child to play the sport he wants to play, and force him to choose another sport which they prefer.

The choice very often falls on a particular discipline because it is thought to be socially desirable. In other circumstances, it is the parent's personal passion that conditions the child towards a certain activity. In other cases, parents fear that the sport chosen by the child may be too violent and, therefore, the choice falls on a less demanding discipline. On other occasions, the choice may be determined only on the basis of convenience - maybe because there is a soccer field or gym near home, while the child's preference would mean having to face transportation problems and difficulties.

Due to all these situations the child may appear to be disinterested and highly de-motivated while playing his sports activity and may therefore tend to live his sports experience more like a constriction rather than a real pleasure. This is because he will work and dedicate his time to sport more for his parent's sake than for his own. The child should never consider sport as a means to enforce his relationship with his parents.

The child should personally decide what sport he would like to play, because only in this case will he be able to fully express his own personality and potential and therefore considerably benefit at an educational level as well.

Fulvio Bernardini - a famous coach - once stated, in a purely provocative manner, that coaching orphan youth players would be the ideal solution for a team coach. In this way it would be possible to avoid dangerous intrusions on the part of the players' parents.

Parents should not interfere with the choices of their children. Their activity should be limited to the task of finding a suitable club and place where their child's favorite activity is taught in the best way possible and where the psychological environment and atmosphere are in perfect harmony with the personal needs of the child. The parents should take care of making the best choice and finding a sports structure and club that especially emphasizes the importance of an overall educational project aimed at helping individual maturation and learning and allowing the youth to freely express his potential skills at the intellectual, physical and social level.

Many teach soccer, but very few are able to provide what each player needs in accordance with his age. For this reason, parents should not take their children to the nearest soccer field just because it is easy and convenient for them to get there. The choice should be mainly based on the educational product that the sports club can offer to the family.

The relationship with the child

The child should be able to draw pleasure from sport. Nobody - and most of all, the parents - should put too much responsibility on the child occupied in any sports activity. The child should be able to win, lose, play well or not, without fearing his parents' reactions.

The parents should neither burden the child with great tension nor give the impression that winning is the main goal. Certain parents would do far better for their child if they could avoid being too intrusive and obsessive, allowing him to play in a condition of total serenity and peace of mind. The child should be encouraged when it becomes evident that he is in trouble and must handle a difficult situation. He should be constantly rewarded even when he makes the slightest progress since this may be extremely important for him. It is fundamental not to put him in a position to compete with his teammates, thus avoiding comparing his results with those of more skillful players. Obviously, this is valid not only for soccer but also for school activities.

It is evident that parents feel proud when their child is amongst the best, but this must not become an obsession. If he loses a match or has not played well, parents should avoid showing disappointment. Otherwise, the child will suffer not only because he has lost the competition, but also because he has disappointed his parents.

Parents who make these errors can be easily recognized amongst those who are always present at their children's training sessions and competitions and typically show clear signs of suffering because they cannot directly take an active part in their children's activity. Occasionally, they even enter in direct conflict with the coach if they are convinced that he is unable to get the best out of their children. If the coach assigns a role or a position other than that which they really expect for their children, or if the child does not play as they would expect. Not to mention all the various situations when the child is totally excluded from the match or confined to the bench. In this case, it is as if the parents themselves were excluded from the competition; this sense of frustration inevitably causes bitter conflicts with the coach. In many cases, parents are inclined to consider the coach's behavior and decisions in a purely irrational way, and their approach generally results from a psychological defensive mechanism whereby the coach becomes the real scapegoat, the only obstacle that prevents their child from achieving success. This is due to the fact that it is dramatically difficult for most parents to acknowledge the limits of their children, while it is much easier to blame the incompetence of the coach.

In reality, this type of parent generally obtains the exact opposite of what he desires. In fact, his child is unlikely to ever become a champion. As a matter of fact, he is very likely to become one of the many young players who abandon sport during adolescence when other interests become predominant. These are the children who often come to resent their parent's intrusions and tend to rebel. Many researchers have demonstrated that motivation to success (or 'achievement' as it is typically defined in America) is strictly dependent on a correct and respectful behavior within the family. For a player to finally become a real champion he needs to grow in a warm and stimulating atmosphere within a family which is able to offer him the support he needs without conditioning his choices.

Parents acting as a support for their children

Studies carried out in the past on top-level players have shown that their parents had played a role of crucial importance in shaping their personal motivations. It clearly emerged that their parents had also played sport at a medium level at least and that they had achieved an excellent degree of personal achievement.

Those researches also showed that their parents had introduced their children to sport, but not necessarily to the sport they had played. They were able to understand the progress their children were making in sport and generally considered their sports experiences as a means to elevate their children's prestige and, partly, regain prestige themselves.

Researches also helped to find out that the parents of those players who finally reached high levels rewarded the progress made by their children in sport and also constantly supported them at an economic, moral and emotional level.

A top-level athlete generally has a well-balanced family background characterized by marked sports tradition. Technical possibilities are conditioned by feelings of insecurity and lack of personal motivations which inevitably result from inadequate psycho-pedagogical solutions. Personal aspirations - and young players' ambitions in particular - are inhibited or exasperated by parents' needs. It is very difficult for a young player to make important and decisive choices when the models and life styles suggested by his coach are in conflict with those he is offered by his parents.

The type of relationship obviously becomes very important when the child truly has the ability to achieve success. There are young players who are thought to be potential champions when they are only ten or eleven years old thanks to their individual skills. When a parent has a highly skillful and talented child, he should not commit the error of making him feel different from his teammates. Rather, he should do his best to limit the messages coming from the outside world which may suggest to the young soccer player the impression that he is exceptionally gifted. Most parents transfer their hopes and dreams to their children. If a child is convinced at an early age that his talent sets him apart from the rest of the team, his motivation to improve will inevitably suffer.

Parents should immediately realize that their skillful child must be treated like any other child of his age group who does not have the same talent and skills. School must be the primary objective even for a highly talented child; parents should never think that school can be neglected in favor of sport for the good of the child.

Too many factors determine success in soccer, too many are those who have dreamed of achieving success and afterwards regretted they did not hold a diploma. Only a very small minority can finally achieve success in soccer and play as professional players; the others must search for self-fulfillment in other aspects of life. When sport is interpreted in the wrong way, it can cause psychological suffering and a deep sense of loneliness; this is exactly what parents should understand.

The relationship with the club. Parents should also be willing to cooperate with the club. They should realize that a discrete presence in the clubís life can be very useful, especially in an environment where voluntary service is the focal point of the whole sports experience.

In particular, parents should be present when the club holds special meetings, so that they may be informed of the social activities and all those programs which directly concern their children. Parents should constantly communicate with the club and support their activity. Mutual dialogue, however, should not become a sort of 'seductive' approach towards club managers and coaching staff with the hopes of obtaining some advantages for their children.

If, on one hand, excessively intrusive parents seem to be the greatest problem for both the coach and the club, today some parents even dare to consider the club only as a nursery for their children. Youth soccer schools are often thought to play this role and, consequently, parents are firmly persuaded that their being interested in their children's sports activity is of little or no use in the learning process of their children.

This lack of interest very often results from a typical form of egotism, so that parents tend to delegate to others important educational responsibilities which they should personally take towards their children.

THE REFEREE

Much has been said about soccer referees, but very little has been written. The referee is certainly the 'least loved' figure in soccer, even though he is undoubtedly the most talked about. No match ends without supporters, club managers, sports journalists and players putting the referee and his performance under discussion. Paradoxically, the person who is designated to make players comply with the rules of the game too often becomes the most discussed character in the soccer performance.

But who is the referee in reality? What leads him to face such a difficult task week by week? What are his motivations?

Many have tried to give an answer to these questions, but we can easily say that little has been done to try to deeply understand who the man in the black shirt who dares to handle twenty-two brightly dressed players and struggles to impose the rules of the game really is. The referee is so unpopular because both players and supporters feel that he is the major obstacle to the final success of the match. The need to make a successful score inevitably induces not only the athlete but also the supporter to forget that the final result in soccer cannot leave aside the respect for the rules of the game.

The referee plays the typical role of a leader: and as a leader he is inevitably identified by players and spectators as well. His authority is based on special organizational needs and on a proxy that is officially granted by the federal board, without players expressing their personal consent. Consequently, the referee is directly chosen neither by players nor by supporters, he is imposed from the outside.

In many cases, the error is made in youth soccer of appointing the least skillful players as referees. This helps to favor the traditional mentality that unconsciously associates the referee with a poorly skilled or incompetent person. Consequently, it is easy to understand why he usually finds it very difficult to be accepted by players, supporters and so forth in the same way as all those set rules preventing freedom of choice are typically viewed in a completely negative light.

The sole fact that he is dressed in black makes him seem different from those beloved heroes playing in brilliant and colored shirts. The color black usually triggers heavy negative association mechanisms so that the individual is inevitably encouraged to associate this color with particular social roles that are typically considered in a negative light - like magistrates, policemen, and even priests for instance. These are all social figures who have the tough responsibility of judging the actions of human beings. Furthermore, black typically symbolizes mourning and this certainly does not encourage a positive attitude. Furthermore, those who have a difficult relationship with authorities in general are more inclined to transfer this conflict to their relations with the referee, projecting all their aggressiveness on him during the course of the competition.

However, it is also fundamental to try to understand the person hiding behind his black jacket. It is important to consider the referee in a different light, as the twenty-third athlete entering the playing field, and to carefully analyze all the various technical, athletic, physiological, medical and also psychological aspects that directly concern this crucial figure in soccer.

Recruiting and selection

The world of referees also involves recruiting and selection. The referee association and structure in Italy is a highly efficient body that is able to successfully handle a very impressionable phenomenon every week-end. Suffice to think of the thousands of matches that are regularly played on Saturdays and Sundays on the playing fields throughout Italy. In reality, it is not so easy to recruit young people willing to dedicate their time to refereeing. Widespread prejudice considerably limits the number of those who would try this experience.

Selections in various towns throughout Italy aim at recruiting young players for a special course for new referees. Unfortunately, the number of referees that are really needed, especially for the activity at the youth level, is still inadequate.

Maybe we should try to find more stimulating solutions and incentives, or stipulate that those who want to become soccer coaches must first experience a stage period as referees at the youth level. This last possibility would not only provide coverage for many games at the youth level, but could also offer another significant advantage at the professional level, since those coaches who want to become referees should perfectly know the rules of the game and above all directly learn how difficult it is to make correct decisions in a fraction of a second. As far as recruitment is concerned, the selection should obviously favor those who interpret the role of the referee as a sport, those who are strongly motivated towards sport so that their personal interests and motivations may boost their desire to constantly improve themselves both in technical and environmental terms. Those who suffer from serious psychological problems resulting from their difficult relationship with themselves should not be recruited to play the role of referee. In fact, those who are motivated to become referees only because they will feel important wearing a uniform and having a whistle in their mouths will inevitably fail sooner or later.

Personal motivations

From a psychological point of view it is important to understand the reasons and the motivations that generally encourage a person to embark on such a hard experience as refereeing. A research carried out by professors Maderna and Fiorone on 44 referees working in Premiership and First Division some years ago clearly showed their most deeply felt motivations included a strong need to emerge and be noted and a desire to escape from a gray daily routine.

A strong desire to overcome personal feelings of insecurity through notoriety, the applause of the masses and total independence in decision making was generally suggested as a second motivational drive.

In 1992, we carried out a significant research distributing a ready-made questionnaire to about 250 referees working in amateur leagues. Our study was aimed at getting some more information that could help us to understand a bit more about the referee as an individual, about his problems and fears. As far as the motivational aspect was concerned, they clearly indicated they had decided to embark on this kind of activity mainly because it offered them the opportunity to play sport and engage in physical activity.

Another motivational agent, in the order of importance, was the desire to travel and see new places.

At third place, the possibility to meet new people; fourth - it was simply a way for them to spend their leisure time; fifth - a way to ensure an important role; sixth - a means for self-fulfillment outside the sphere of one's job; seventh - a means to escape from family monotony.

That research also helped us to understand that the motivations which generally stimulate a person to become a referee are somewhat similar to those of an athlete. In the role of the referee, like in that of most players, the motivational agent is very frequently connected to individual needs for personal compensation. As a matter of fact, refereeing - which means handling full power while on the playing field - may gratify those who consciously or unconsciously find it particularly difficult to perceive their own personal value and whose self-confidence and esteem are therefore very low. This is why these personalities often engage in activities which involve handling power over other individuals.

The fact that they are directly appointed to special tasks involving control and power over other individuals makes them feel strong and therefore able to counterbalance their deep feelings of inferiority.

A magistrate's gown, a policeman's uniform, a teacher's desk or more simply a guardian's cap often hide fragile personalities who use their jobs as a means to mask or counterbalance their weaknesses. It's clear that these problems may also arise amongst referees and in their relationships to other individuals in particular, as in any other role where power is involved in our social reality.

Anxiety disorders

In the research we have carried out on the above-mentioned 250 referees we have also tried to focus the attention on their personal experiences and their psychological approach to the competition. Like many soccer players who often suffer from serious anxiety disorders in the hours immediately preceding the competition, many referees also have to deal with such critical problems in the pre-match period.

When answering the questionnaires, most of the referees openly admitted that they generally suffered from feelings of inadequacy and psychological tension before any competition.

90% of the referees interviewed in our survey declared they typically suffered from stress- and anxiety-related symptoms - some of them in any situation, others only in the case of a particularly important match.

98% explicitly stated they were willing to learn special muscle relaxation techniques in order to better control anxiety and, consequently, improve their performance.

They were also asked to list the various attributes which, according to them, a referee absolutely needs to reach top-level performances. They clearly indicated, in order of importance: self-confidence, technical skills, athletic conditioning, physical fitness, personal culture and competence and, lastly, recommendations.

The referees' passion for sport also emerged from the fact that the interviewed referees generally play sport 2 to 6 hours a week on average. From the data we have collected in our survey, we get a clear image of a referee who is highly motivated, loves sport and is willing to know and learn whatever may help him to improve his performance. It is therefore necessary to work on these bases bearing in mind the intent to make this activity 'more human' integrating it more and more in our complex soccer system.

The general sense of anxiety that most referees feel before a competition is the same as that of a player who is getting ready to enter the playing field. This is why the referee should also learn to include special methods and techniques for suitable psychological conditioning in his general training programs. We have already discussed these problems in the chapter dedicated to the adult soccer player.

Handling the competition

A very popular referee of the past once said that a good referee is one who does not make himself noticed while on the playing field. In reality, he was absolutely right, since a really competent and talented referee is able to handle the competition firmly while avoiding any possible theatrical performance. His task is to ensure that the rules of the game are respected without putting anything personal in his behavior on the field.

The referee should not let himself be psychologically involved in what is happening around him, starting from the players' attitudes towards him, to the general behavior of the supporters, the club managers and the coach as well. When he is on the playing field he must only apply the rules, without being too personally involved in what is going on around him. Personal experience will slowly help the referee to understand that even the worst offenses that he may receive while working are not cutting remarks made about him as an individual, but about the role he is playing at that moment. Consequently, his role is a sort of 'body armor' that he can use to protect his most intimate feelings.

If a referee could keep this concept clear in his mind, he could maintain great lucidity and total serenity on all occasions while working on the playing field. During the competition the referee must also be able to successfully handle possible errors he commits on the field. He often realizes that he has taken a wrong decision. What he should always remember is that if he acts by way of compensation, he may also run the risk of making a second mistake. In order to avoid this, it is important that he accepts the fact that he can make mistakes and that his awareness should not stimulate a psychological state which inevitably favors other errors due to compensation.

His personal approach to the players should also be 'filtered' through his role. The rules of the game firmly offer suitable solutions to any situation. This is why the referee's behavior should not be authoritarian but purely authoritative - which means he must have the capacity to take firm decisions, but without heavily emphasizing his role and power, either verbally or in other manners.

When watching soccer matches either on TV or at stadiums, we can often see anxious officials who display excessively tough behavior towards players. This typically happens when the referee still needs to convince himself of his role, when his personal feelings of insecurity contaminate his official role or when he is afraid he is not up to his task.

THE CLUB MANAGER

The club manager plays a very important role in youth soccer. He is undoubtedly one of the leading figures, particularly in youth soccer, where voluntary service is the engine which allows the whole organization to function. The club manager generally devotes his free time to the organization of that basic soccer activity on which soccer as a whole lays its foundations. Thanks to the interest and the real passion of these people, every year thousands of children can discover the great pleasure of playing soccer, a game that is still the most beautiful sport in the world.

Much has been written about the roles of players, educators and coaches and today, fresh research and authoritative studies on the subject constantly provide us with a lot of useful information concerning the psychological aspects connected to these figures. On the other hand, little has been written about the club manager's role and about the motivations which induced him to choose this activity.

We can easily say that the club manager has been somewhat ignored. It is almost as if he were thought to play a role of minor importance in the achievement of final competitive goals. This is due to the fact that sport was considered to be pure competition and nothing else at all until some years ago. This negligence clearly supported the idea that successful scores in sport could be achieved only by those who directly entered the playing field: that is players, coaches and even the referee to a certain extent.

Today, we are well aware that the time has come for us to better understand the role played by the club manager, also because our social reality has considerably changed and clubs and associations could not but change accordingly. And especially because today we have finally understood that soccer can offer many educational and social advantages that go far beyond purely athletic and competitive scores awarded with cups and trophies.

The club manager of the 90s is certainly different from the fan who could only apply to his love for soccer and his personal intuition as the only instruments to handle a soccer club 30 or 40 years ago. In the same way that both parents and coaches have gradually changed their behaviors and slightly adjusted some particular aspects of their roles in order to develop harmonious relations with the new generations as time went by, the role of the club manager has gradually acquired innovative connotations in order to better understand the needs of the new generation of players.

How the role of the the manager has evolved over time

Over the years, the role of the club manager has undergone significant changes. In the past, he generally identified with the figure of a person who dedicated his free time and invested his money with the sole scope of putting his 'club' in the condition to achieve purely competitive targets.

It was a very difficult job which included planning soccer activity, handling administrative problems and interpersonal relations as well.

Up until the 70s, the strategy of the club was always dictated by the imperative need to win competitions; no difference was made between youth activity and adult soccer, victory was the only important reality!

A youth playing soccer wearing an earring or with his hair tied in a horse-tail no longer makes news today. Only a few years ago, these situations would not have been tolerated. Obviously, the relationships within the soccer club were in line with the social context of that time, a period when the idea of a group with its peculiar principles, dynamics and conflicts was still considered to be of little importance.

Before the 70s, the management's authority was passively accepted within the soccer club and there was little or no open dialogue at all between the various members of the club. The leadership was certainly based on individual authority. The individual was of little importance in the context of the club, and this reality, especially at the youth level, inevitably exasperated selection. Apart from final victory, the ultimate aim was to shape and produce new talent to field in the major teams of the club or to sell to the highest bidder. It was of little importance if the club originally started out with 100 young players and that only 5 of them were finally enrolled in the first team. The number of wins in championship contests as well as the cups and trophies conquered were the only means to define the value of the club and, consequently, the real value of the club management.

Starting from the 70s on, something new began to develop in the soccer clubs. The fall of authoritarian models, as a result of the young peoples' movement in 1968, inevitably brought about a strong need for renewal in the world of soccer as well.

Those young soccer players, children of the general period of social innovation, were no longer willing to passively accept the role of subordinate players, and that widespread feeling of conflict was particularly felt by teenagers. This inevitably brought about serious difficulties in the relations between players, coaches and club managers as a direct consequence of clear changes in the needs of those players who wanted to be increasingly independent and desired to be considered as individuals first rather than players exclusively.

The dramatic effects of that lack of communication were soon evident. Many young players abandoned sport in adolescence. In a study sponsored by the Italian National Olympic Committee and carried out at Padua University it clearly emerged that many young players finally decided to give up sport mainly because they could not stand the authoritarian and totalitarian nature of their clubs. 75% of the players interviewed in our survey even stated that they had to pay great attention while expressing their personal ideas regarding social and political matters.

In Vincenzo Prunelli's popular book "The Soccer Player: training, professional activity, psychological aspects", he writes that only 3 to 4% of the players playing in youth soccer finally made the at first teams; this clearly proves that abandonment is a critical phenomenon that deserves greater attention. The fact that a number of young players give up their sports activity at a very early stage in their playing has obviously caused serious problems and difficulties, so that it has sometimes been practically impossible to create new teams due to a considerable shortage of players. In other cases, some teams even had the number of their players cut to half in the middle of the season so that it was nearly impossible for them to handle the situation.

It is essential that the club manager of the year 2000 be able to understand the characteristics and the needs of the human resources he has at his disposal in order to avoid unpleasant situations. Certainly, modern club managers, and especially the managers in the future, should display great competence in successfully handling interpersonal relationships. Modern competent managers are those who finally manage to include their clubs and experiences in the general social background. When this occurs, it also helps the manager himself to improve at a cultural level.

The manager running the youth soccer club must be perfectly aware that his club should aim at something other than purely competitive goal. In certain urban districts, youth soccer clubs may act as real elements of aggregation aimed at helping young players to overcome social and psychological maladjustment.

Secondly, a competent and modern manager should understand that a child who is selected to play in his team today must first of all learn to know himself, his body, the pleasure and all the various possibilities that motor activity can offer. Unlike what usually happened in the past, children have fewer opportunities to have spontaneous physical exercise today and are therefore still unable to fully exploit their body potential when they begin to play in youth soccer teams. Before 'building' the soccer player, one should first of all think of shaping the human being. These are the main aspects which modern and competent club managers should especially focus their attention on. They must be able to patiently wait for the young players to grow and mature and consequently avoid thinking that coaches are absolutely incompetent or unable to perform their tasks if they cannot achieve successful results within a short period of time.

The modern manager should feel gratified when he sees that young players are first of all happy to play soccer in a serene environment and gradually learn to discover the pleasure of motor activity and passion for sport. Coaches who are appointed to younger teams should display great competence in dealing with basic motor training, stimulating and motivating young players through a suitable emotional and affective approach.

The club manager should always act shrewdly before making each decision, trying to carefully analyze the coaches he has at his disposal and understanding and finally selecting those who could best run each team because of their technical skills and personalities. As we have already said regarding coaches working with youth players, it is fundamental to forget the traditional idea that the last coach on board should necessarily be appointed to coaching the youngest team, while the oldest coach should be in charge of the most important team in the club. This assumption is definitely out-of-date, since it is first of all fundamental to favor the coaches' individual attitudes and personal dispositions: this means that every coach should be put in a position to coach those players who best match his human, relational and professional attributes.

Another important aspect concerning the role of the modern club manager engaged in youth soccer is his relationship with parents. The manager should favor interpersonal relationships, mutual discussion and open dialogue between coaches and players' parents within the club. As a matter of fact, it is extremely important that all those figures operating around the child use the same educational model so as to approach the athlete in the same way.

Very often the coaching staff and the child's parents are unable to carry out the same educational program and this inevitably creates confusion and bewilderment in the child. The manager of a youth soccer club should therefore encourage mutual communication between the coaching staff and players' parents so that they can share common intents in their educational approach. The ideal solution would be to involve school too, so as to carry out a common educational program.

Club strategies and programs

An increasingly strong need is spreading out in soccer according to which clear-cut programs, schedules and goals are the necessary basis on which youth soccer clubs should build their activity. Working without clear ideas and principles and without the means and instruments that are needed to achieve a final goal is certainly the first thing to avoid when running a soccer club.

Suitable planning practically implies the ability to understand and foresee what will happen in the future and consequently study the path to follow, the intermediate steps to take accordingly, and the means and the instruments needed to verify both the quality and quantity of what has been done.

Consequently, it is first of all necessary for a club to set their final goals and design the strategies they are going to implement in order to achieve their purposes.

The real meaning of suitable planning must therefore be seen from a larger perspective, as a means to finally achieve the goals which have been previously set. It's clear that setting special club strategies and schedules should not be seen as something magical, as a talisman that allows us to finally get to any kind of much longed-for target. Both the final targets and the aims of the club and the people working in the club must be compatible with the means the club has at its disposal and therefore be connected to the external social reality in which the club exists.

It is obvious that it would be too complicated, and even inopportune, to set strict programs for soccer clubs. We cannot forget that most of them are mainly based on voluntary service and do not have well-organized management structures.

We are firmly convinced that the main stages for a simple planning process in youth soccer should include:
- careful analysis of the external social background
- setting and defining general goals
- setting and defining specific objectives
- quantification of both general and specific objectives
- approval
- final evaluation.

Careful analysis of the external social background

This means that a suitable planning process should begin with a careful analysis of the situation and the general background in which the club is growing.

Such factors as political, economic and demographic situations should all be taken into proper account. The relations with the affiliated governing body (USYSA, AYSO ...) will allow us to know the number of soccer clubs developing in a certain district, the number of players and, if necessary, the need to further enhance such activity in that particular area.

The external environment is also made up of other important structures (playing fields and gyms, for instance) and it is therefore important to know their availability and organization, the opening hours and rent costs. From the administrative and legal point of view, it is important to know whether the club can be granted funds in the form of special sports grants or other loans lent by local companies or banks.

The economic situation should also be taken into proper account in order to find out if there are companies who are interested in sponsoring the club's activity. Both the social reality and the environmental situation generally deserve great attention. As a matter of fact, a club developing in a small country environment certainly has a different background compared to that of a club developing in the heart or on the outskirts of a big city.

Great attention should also be focused on such aspects as juvenile delinquency, unemployment and social marginalization, especially with the support of the data collected and the information provided by public bodies and associations in general.

Setting and defining general goals.

The expression 'general objectives' refers to the strategic lines that the club intends to follow. They may concern the number of potential players the club intends to recruit and introduce to their sport in a certain period of time (in one year or within a few years, for instance) or the relationships they are going to develop with both the schools and all the other associations that are present in the area.

In play, general goals typically define the main working strategy of the club. In fact, the reality today is completely different compared to the situation in the past. Until some years ago, the strategies of most soccer clubs were based on the principle of bitter competition exclusively, while the rest was of little or no interest at all.

Attention was mainly focused on winning competitions and shaping youth champions who could be sold to elite soccer clubs so as to earn large amounts of money. These types of clubs still exist today, but a wide range of smaller clubs have gradually developed in the last few years that mainly intend to emphasize the idea that soccer should be considered as an educational tool they can offer to our society. In general, these clubs are not that interested in creating great players.

These modern clubs generally aim at favoring any form of leisure and aggregation activity mainly intended as an instrument to prevent juvenile delinquency and discomfort. They typically try to avoid any exaggeratedly selective implications and usually apply to purely educational methods for coaching soccer. In other words, for these clubs the individual is definitely more important than the soccer player.

Setting and defining specific objectives
Compared to the above-mentioned general goals, specific objectives can include special technical, organizational and financial targets. Winning a league, being promoted to a higher division, being registered in a provincial or regional league may be indicated as specific objectives in a typically 'traditional' club - as can be the ability of a club to fully exploit fresh talent.

A club which is particularly interested in educational matters may set specific goals like constantly stimulating great interest among young players, rewarding and therefore attracting as many players as possible to the club, so as to cut the number of those who decide to abandon soccer.

Specific objectives may also be connected to the need of the club to grow at the economic level by means of sponsoring activity, income from soccer camps and profits coming from running tournaments and other events. Important specific objectives also include active participation on the part of all those persons who are somehow involved in the activity of the club. Particular attention should be focused on the parents' relationship to the club and on their personal approach to sport as well.

Quantification of both general and specific objectives
Quantification of both general and specific goals should be tied to the real potential of the club as well as to their human and economic resources.

The sure way to make mistakes is to set unrealistic goals that soon appear to be impossible to achieve. The greater their objectives, the more the club should have a really solid economic basis and the more they should recruit human resources that are willing to dedicate their free time to this activity. Selecting and recruiting the coaching staff is surely a very delicate specific objective that consequently deserves careful study and great attention - as a matter of fact, making mistakes in this field may even upset or hinder the whole planning process. This means that coaches should not be selected simply because they are popular figures, but because they share the club's philosophy and planning strategy.

Approval
A modern soccer club should be conceived as a group of highly motivated people working together to achieve special goals. Obviously, a group of people working together for the same aim also means a combination of different ways of thinking, of ideas that are often in conflict with each other as well as a variety of individual personalities.

Freedom of thought, open dialogue, fair discussion and mutual confrontation on several ideas and the best ways to carry out well-defined plans should be constantly favored within the club. This means that the management should openly communicate their programs and the objectives they intend to pursue - all the better if such plans and targets are also accepted by all those people who somehow play an active role in the club (management, coaching staff, players, parents.). It is important that those who are interested in the activity of the club all deal with such important matters and regularly discuss both plans and goals.

Sharing common objectives is the first rule to follow in order to finally achieve them. Conflicts and feelings of hostility - especially if they are not openly expressed - generally increase the tension between the parties, seriously impairing interpersonal relationships in some cases. It is advisable to accurately distribute roles and assignments in order to avoid over-lapping of roles, which could bring about conflicts and disputes in the long term. It is also important to find the best way to reward those people who constantly work hard as volunteers in the club.

Moreover, parents should take an active part in the activity of the club: for instance, they should be personally involved in meetings that may also act as moments of convivial pleasure. Conferences and meetings may also become suitable occasions for the club to communicate their strategies and plans so as to make sure that they are shared and accepted by the families.

Final evaluation

The final evaluation of what has been done and achieved during the course of the soccer season is a moment of critical importance in the reality of the club and should therefore be included in the club's planning process. The club board should meet several times throughout the season in order to make partial evaluations of the work done and therefore adjust those strategies that did not prove effective in achieving set goals. Final evaluation should be made at the end of the whole cycle; this is the right time to carefully assess the situation. As we have already pointed out, the cycle can cover a period of one year, but most clubs today use longer cycles covering a period of about two or three soccer seasons.

Club managers' personal motivations

The club manager, like all those belonging to the world of soccer, should be perfectly aware of the reasons and personal motivations that stimulate him to dedicate his free time to this activity.

Since no special studies or works have ever been published concerning club managers' personal motivations, we thought it advisable to carry out a basic survey on the main factors that encourage a person to embark on such a difficult job. For this survey, we distributed special ready-made questionnaires to a number of club managers. In this way, we could easily understand their conscious and unconscious motivations, that is all those inner motivational drives that are not generally perceived by the subject, but inevitably condition his behavior.

In order to identify and understand subconscious motivations it would be necessary to use special psychometric tests: we plan to use this method of research in the near future.

Our questionnaire was distributed to 100 people working in youth soccer, basketball and swimming. It was made up of a list of 10 motivational factors, each one involving a scale of values ranging from 1 to 5 and defining the intensity of each specific agent. Here are the 10 motivational factors included in the questionnaire:
- feeling young
- remaining in the world of sport as long as possible
- escaping from the family routine
- dissatisfaction at work
- a way to spend leisure time
- playing a role of critical importance
- desire to meet new people
- desire to dedicate oneself to young players
- desire to travel
- economic advantage.

We decided to include these ten factors in the questionnaire and exclude other motivations after talking with the selected managers at the various (but still too few) meetings and special courses for club managers run by regional federations. Careful analysis of the answers gave us a sufficiently clear idea as to the main reasons and factors that typically encouraged those interviewed managers to engage in such a tough job.

From a careful reading of the questionnaires, it clearly emerged that 'desire to dedicate oneself to young people' was the motivational factor that got the highest score. 78% of the interviewees attributed 5 points (the highest level) to this factor, while 12% assigned 4 points and 10% 3 points. In short, this motivational factor clearly got the highest score with a total of 468 points.

The information we accumulated can therefore be summed up as follows: as we have just said above, the first factor was the desire to help young people; the second was the possibility to remain in the world of sport as long as possible; third: the possibility to meet new people; fourth: it is simply a way to spend free time; fifth: the desire to travel; sixth: a way to feel young and avoid psychological aging; seventh: personal dissatisfaction in the working environment; eighth: the opportunity to play an important role; ninth: the possibility to get economic profit; and tenth: the desire to escape from family routine.

These results should help us to carefully consider such a critical problem as personal motivation. The results of our survey should be considered only as a starting point and act as a stimulus for further investigation and more detailed and comprehensive research. Actually, certain themes like 'the possibility to get economic profit' and 'a way to escape from family routine' obviously deserve greater attention and should be further investigated through special psychological tests.

Personal motivational factors inevitably evolve and change as time goes by. Maybe, the fact that it is extremely difficult to recruit people who are willing to dedicate their time to sport and work as volunteers in sports associations today clearly suggests how personal interests are constantly changing. In the past, these people could easily be rewarded for their help with a dinner or a gift offered at the end of the season; now, a simple gift or a dinner are no longer enough and clubs should carefully reflect upon this reality.

Hopefully, clubs at all levels will focus greater attention on the role played by the club manager in the future, since the club manager is certainly the focal point around which much of the soccer activity revolves. It may be necessary to increase the number and enhance the quality of the special training courses for club managers but, above all, it would be advisable to begin to carefully study this important figure that obviously deserves greater attention in the world of soccer.

SUPPORTERS AND SPECTATORS

Both in Europe and South America soccer is undoubtedly the most popular sport. Many believe that soccer has achieved such a great success because of its peculiar features: it is a team game, the rules of the game are quite simple, it can be played by anybody and anywhere, it can easily attract an incredible number of supporters and spectators and so forth. In fact, these factors and other important aspects have gradually helped soccer to become such a popular sport to the point that it is now a mass phenomenon. Many have talked and written about soccer: much has been written about the stories of its heroes, its myths and their performances to the point that the soccer phenomenon was finally defined a social and economic event.

The soccer phenomenon has now become a form of religion in our modern culture. Stadiums are its temples, players are its clergymen while supporters are its followers. The soccer game is a ritual, a ceremony that takes place every week-end, that is advertised and carefully prepared during the week through lively discussions and the reading of those ìHoly Scripturesî that are sports journals and newspapers. Some may not approve that soccer is compared to religion, but if we carefully reflect upon the emotional implications and the real psychological exasperation that this phenomenon involves, we can easily see that many perceive soccer as a creed and for some even represents the only real source of interest in their lives. Soccer was and is still so popular in our society because it is able to attract the interest of thousands of people, while also gratifying some of their needs.

However, soccer intended as a mass phenomenon is seriously ill today, suffering from a disease called violence. This is a very serious problem that will certainly cause an increasingly large number of potential players or even spectators and supporters to lose interest in the sport if no suitable attention is given to the question. Actually, in the last few years we have realized that many spectators and supporters prefer to desert stadiums for fear of accidents which too often occur before, during and after soccer competitions.

Spectacular events - especially aimed at satisfying the people's needs, while also arousing public consent and approval - have always characterized the history of man in different forms according to various cultures where they developed.

In Roman times, fights between gladiators typically awoke the interest and passionate enthusiasm of our ancestors. Competitions between teams of gladiators actually allowed the Roman citizens to discharge and relieve aggressiveness in a licit way, through a process of personal identification - a mental process whereby one attributes to oneself the behaviors and thoughts of another person or a group of individuals or a mechanism whereby one emotionally lives other people's experiences as one's own. This was how the Romans were allowed to relieve their tensions; today soccer has somehow replaced those competitions between gladiators, thus becoming the modern means to relieve personal aggressiveness.

According to Desmond Morris, soccer unconsciously symbolizes hunting, that is a situation where both teams play the role of the hunter or the prey alternatively. The heart of the prey is represented by the goal, while the ball may be considered as an arrow shot into the vital part of the victim.

The supporter, who cannot take a really active part in the competition, identifies himself with one of the two teams and therefore transfers their behaviors directly on himself. In this way, he manages to relieve part of his tension and discharge aggressiveness through the movements, actions and behaviors of his favorites on the playing field.

This form of projective identification is a mechanism whereby one expels from oneself and transfers on to another person (or thing), attributes, feelings or objects which one may refuse to acknowledge to oneself. Consequently, soccer helps to release, through emotional participation, those aggressive elements which would be discharged in other situations of everyday life otherwise. I would say that soccer has gradually built its fortune on these important psychological mechanisms. However, modern soccer must deal with the problem of violence that has reached dramatically worrying levels in the last few years; only in this way can the world of soccer get out of this critical situation.

The supporter

The word 'supporter' in sport typically identifies a person who regularly follows a team or an athlete, their performances, is happy for a victory and sad for a defeat.

A few years ago, the International Olympic Committee defined the formula for the perfect supporter. He should:

1) applaud with the same enthusiasm both the winner and the loser;
2) avoid any prejudice towards particular clubs or countries;

3) respect the verdict of the jury or the referee, even when he does not agree with their decision;
4) be able to learn something both from a victory and from a defeat;
5) act with dignity during any sports event (also when his team is playing) and always maintain correct and fair behavior, both inside and outside the stadium.

Unfortunately, these rules seem to be purely academic if we consider what occurs every Sunday before, during and after soccer matches. In the past, little violence developed in stadiums: until some years ago, violent behaviors were generally limited to quarrels, bad words, or slaps in some particular cases, but everything immediately ended when the match was over and peace was promptly restored.

Unfortunately, the reality has changed today. Violence is increasingly spreading out everywhere to the point that stadiums and the surrounding areas have been transformed into real battlefields.

But what is happening in reality? Why have things degraded so much? In reality, soccer has not changed so much as a game. Undoubtedly, the heroes of soccer are much richer because the phenomenon has become more and more a business activity, and the speed of play has considerably increased, just like the rhythm of our everyday lives. Nevertheless, these reasons are not enough to explain so much violence in the world of sport. The point is that the spectator has changed and his mental attitude and approach have changed above all.

Today, the supporter feels that he is personally involved in the soccer match he is watching. He sees his favorite team as a private and personal affair, as an extension of his own personality. The win or loss of his favorite team inevitably becomes his own personal victory or defeat.

The most enthusiastic supporters are those who are unable to put a limit between themselves and their team; consequently, whatever interferes with the performance of their favorite team and hinders its success becomes a potential personal enemy. Both the referee and the opposing supporters are seen as enemies. In many cases, when their favorite team is passing through a negative period, the coach, the president and even the players are also seen as enemies because they are all thought to be responsible for the failure of the whole team.

The identification process whereby the supporter identifies himself with his favorite team has become more and more sophisticated today, so that the supporter no longer has useful servo-mechanisms or inner critical processes that help him to control his feelings, emotions and behaviors.

In general, teenagers account for the largest part of violent supporters, since the desire to transgress set rules is particularly strong during adolescence and has always been a constant component in the life of most young players. As a matter of fact, during this critical period of their lives teenagers cannot properly perceive their own identity. Identity means the awareness of one's own personality and individuality, that is the awareness of playing a role which is commonly acknowledged at a social level.

This is a problem that may often arise in adults who live difficult situations like the unemployed or those who are not fully satisfied with their working activities and private lives. It is exactly in this difficult atmosphere that obsessive enthusiasm and fanaticism on the part of many supporters typically develops. If some time ago these people could easily find other ways to relieve their sense of dissatisfaction (through political or religious interests, for instance), today the crisis of these basic points of reference has gradually helped to direct aggressiveness and repressed energies towards soccer.

Those persons who do not have a well-defined identity are likely to fall in the perverse mechanism of projecting their personal identity on a soccer team or a particular player. Their projective identification often becomes so strong that they live any failure or defeat of their favorite team as their own failure: a defeat that seriously affects the innermost depths of their individual personality. Moreover, these fans also feel it important to be considered an integrating part of a group and therefore share a common group identity - the phenomenon of organized supporters could be seen as a way of satisfying such a strong need.

According to professor Ferrarotti, "The love for soccer clearly suggests the individual's need to engage in a common cause, raise a common banner, and share common ideas and intents".

A person who does not feel an integrating part of any social group may search for self-fulfillment in his playing an active role in a group of violent supporters. As a matter of fact, this could give him a well-defined identity; otherwise, he would feel alone and useless. The needs and inner motivations of these violent supporters obviously originate from their inability to answer the question: who am I? And the more these supporters feel they are criticized, feared and attacked, the more their desire to feel important is satisfied. Furthermore, we should also remember that a good part of the actions taken to curb violence in soccer have achieved very poor results and even opposite effects in some cases. There is no doubt that violent supporters generally need to act in an affectedly theatrical manner, and therefore need to attract the attention of the public opinion on their actions and behaviors. It is also true that the world of soccer bears full responsibility in boosting the phenomenon of supporters to extreme levels.

On the other hand, the most excited supporters obviously feel even more important and involved in soccer when they hear coaches, players and even club managers state that supporters are the twelfth player on the playing field or that playing at home is much easier than playing away. The world of soccer has unconsciously helped to create the supporters phenomenon in the light of the final score. In fact, it is not by chance that we talk of 'folklore' when speaking of supporters. Fans everywhere are constantly dreaming up new spectacular strategies and displays designed to outdo their opposition's supporters.

Today, we can say that the match is first played on the terraces rather than on the playing field. Consequently, it is obvious that the more we talk about this phenomenon and both the television and the press focus the attention on supporters, the more we unconsciously satisfy the needs of these social misfits who search for a role in our society through violent behaviors and the more we enhance their desire to become protagonists.

The problem of violence in soccer does not only concern the police order but should also be faced as a real cultural matter. Sport was originally conceived as a leisure activity and not as a social activity in the most inclusive sense of the word; sport has always been considered as a means and never as an end.

This critical situation is clearly represented in the world of school where the attention and time dedicated to sports culture has always been inadequate compared to the needs of the young players and especially to the educational potential of motor activity in general. All in all, soccer has always been used as an instrument for social control in Italy; suffice to think of all those cases where politicians have used soccer as an instrument to get personal profit. As a matter of fact, we are offered many examples of important politicians running famous clubs or big political parties applying to soccer technical vocabulary in order to seduce potential voters and gain their favor.

However, similar situations also existed in the past: as the Romans could relieve their tensions watching tough fights between gladiators, today supporters can find personal satisfaction watching displays of virtuosity by their favorite players.

The spectator

Fortunately, soccer does not attract only the type of people we have described in the previous paragraph. As a matter of fact, most people can still consider soccer as a show. This type of spectator usually does not experience in the soccer competition in a fully anxious manner as the fanatic supporter typically does. These people generally go to the stadium in order to enjoy themselves, to see a spectacular sports performance together with other individuals. Their approach to sport in general and their relation to soccer in particular does not imply anything else. No psychological compensation mechanisms are activated in this case which make them perceive the soccer event as something absolutely personal.

Fans who play soccer or played in the past generally belong to this category. Players and former players have personally lived the sports experience and can therefore invest in the competition the importance and value it really deserves, without making it an event of critical importance.

These fans merely love soccer as a sports performance, are able to appreciate both its technical and athletic contents and are more or less motivated to watch a soccer match in the same way as if they were enjoying a theatrical play. This method of approaching soccer matches may seem somewhat aseptic, but it is only amongst these people that we can find the real soccer connoisseurs, those who can read and understand all the various technical and tactical implications as they are not blind with passion for one single team. Many of these fair supporters have gradually abandoned stadiums in the last few years in order to avoid jeopardizing their personal safety. Many elderly people and common persons who really enjoyed going to the stadium, maybe accompanied by their wives and children, have been forced to change the way they typically spend their Sunday afternoons.

Little has been done for these people. Soccer clubs cannot understand that it is imperative to restore safety, peace and serenity in stadiums if they don't want to finally lose these spectators. Nobody ever mentions this type of supporter. Clubs typically complain that their spectators continue to decrease in number, but have not understood that special areas within the stadium should be reserved for these people exclusively. There are many fair and enthusiastic supporters who cannot afford to pay the price for a ticket in the grand stand; they could only afford a ticket in the popular terraces, but sitting in this area of the stadium could often mean jeopardizing their own personal safety.

Coaching Books from REEDSWAIN

#785:
Complete Books of Soccer Restart Plays
by Mario Bonfanti and Angelo Pereni
$14.95

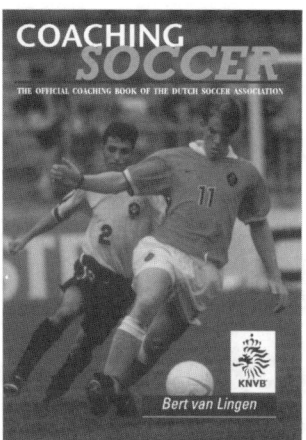

#154:
Coaching Soccer
by Bert van Lingen
$14.95

#177:
PRINCIPLES OF Brazilian Soccer
by José Thadeu Goncalves in cooperation with Prof. Julio Mazzei
$16.95

#185:
Conditioning for Soccer
Dr. Raymond Verheijen
$19.95

#244:
Coaching the 4-4-2
by Maziali and Mora
$14.95

#765:
Attacking Schemes and Training Exercises
by Eugenio Fascetti and Romedio Scaia
$14.95

Call REEDSWAIN 1-800-331-5191

Coaching Books from REEDSWAIN

#786:
Soccer Nutrition
by Enrico Arcelli
$10.95

#788:
ZONE PLAY:
A Tactical and Technical Handbook
$14.95

#267:
Developing Soccer Players
THE DUTCH WAY
$12.95

#175:
The Coaching Philosophies of
Louis van Gaal
and the
Ajax Coaches
by Kormelink and Seeverens
$14.95

#284:
The Dutch Coaching Notebook
$14.95

#287:
Team Building
by Kormelink and Seeverens
$9.95

Web Site: www.reedswain.com

Coaching Books from REEDSWAIN

#291:
Soccer Fitness Training
*by Enrico Arcelli
and Ferretto Ferretti*
$12.95

#261:
Match Analysis
and Game Preparation
Henny Kormelink and Tjeu Seevrens
$12.95

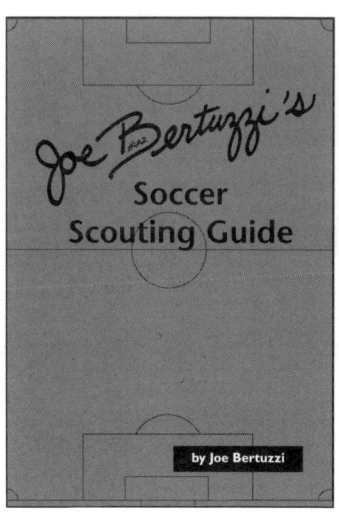

#789:
Soccer Scouting Guide
by Joe Bertuzzi
$12.95

#264:
Coaching
6 to 10 Year Olds
by Giuliano Rusca
$14.95

1-800-331-5191 • www.reedswain.com

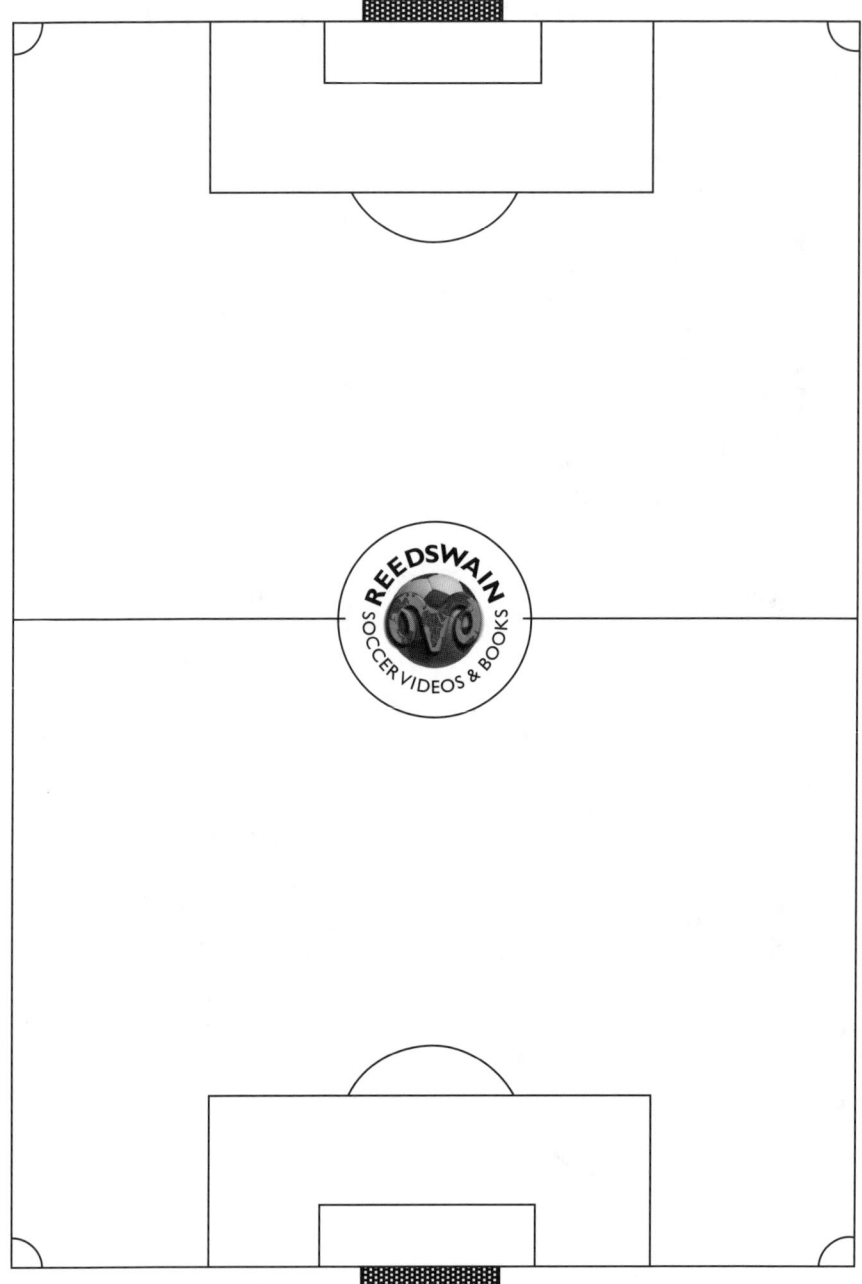

REEDSWAIN INC
612 Pughtown Road
Spring City, Pennsylvania 19475
1-800-331-5191 • **www.reedswain.com**

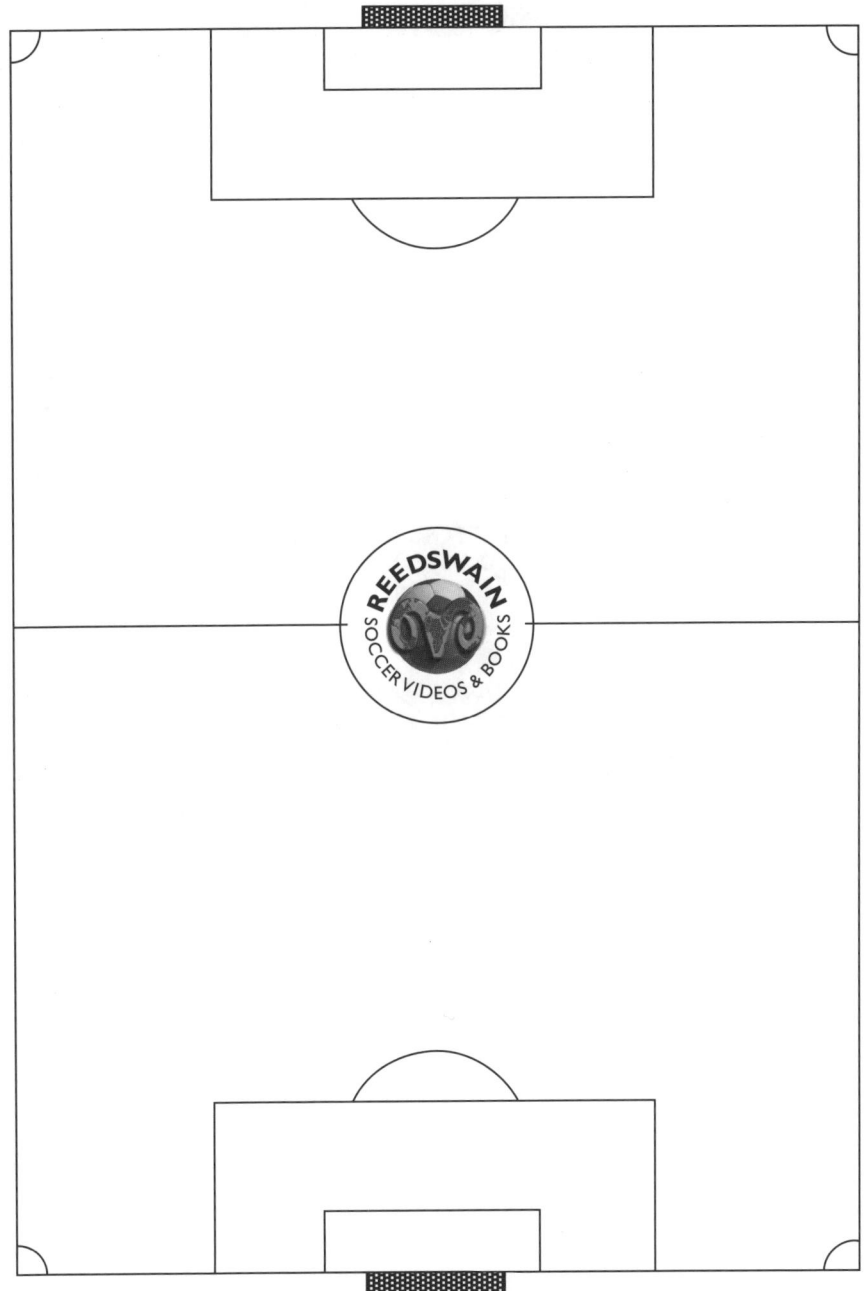

REEDSWAIN INC
612 Pughtown Road
Spring City, Pennsylvania 19475
1-800-331-5191 • **www.reedswain.com**

REEDSWAIN INC
612 Pughtown Road
Spring City, Pennsylvania 19475
1-800-331-5191 • **www.reedswain.com**

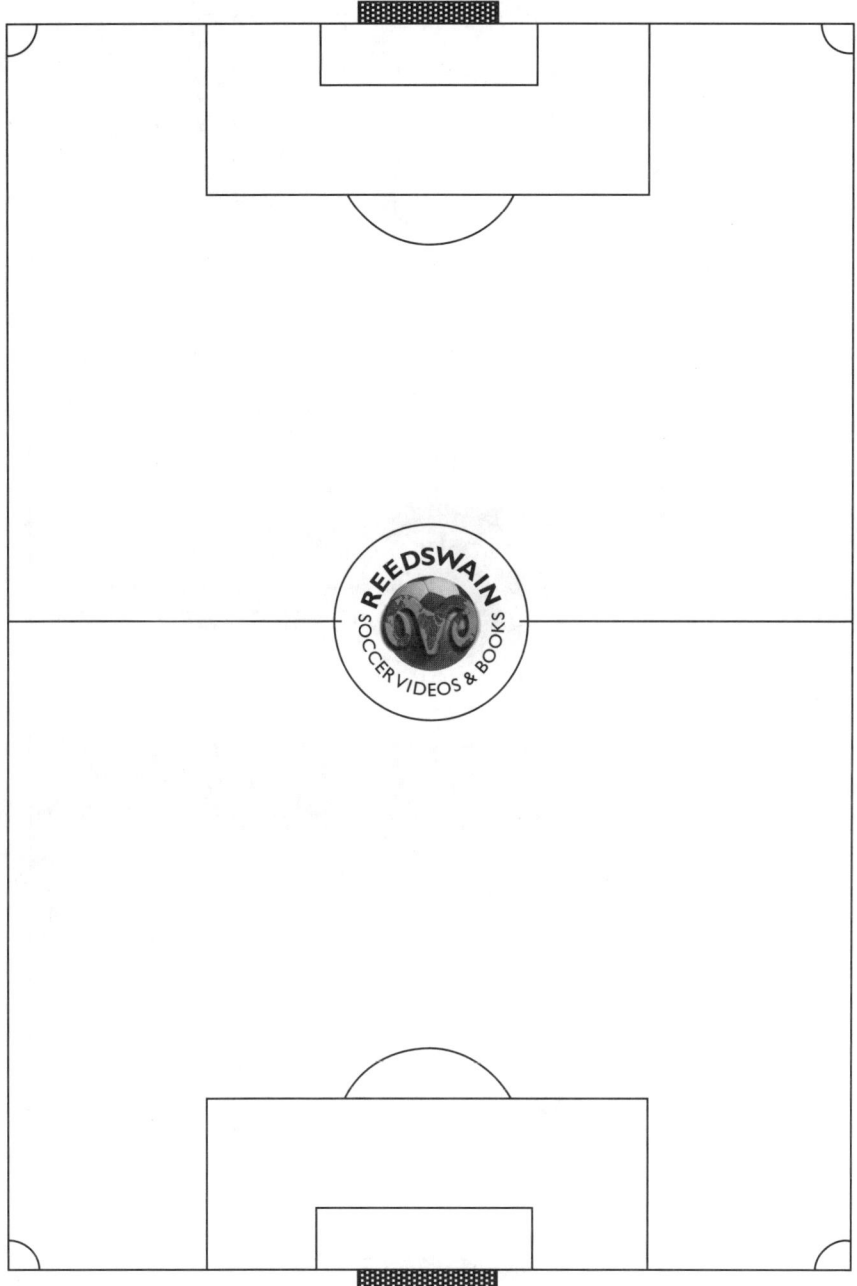

REEDSWAIN INC
612 Pughtown Road
Spring City, Pennsylvania 19475
1-800-331-5191 • www.reedswain.com

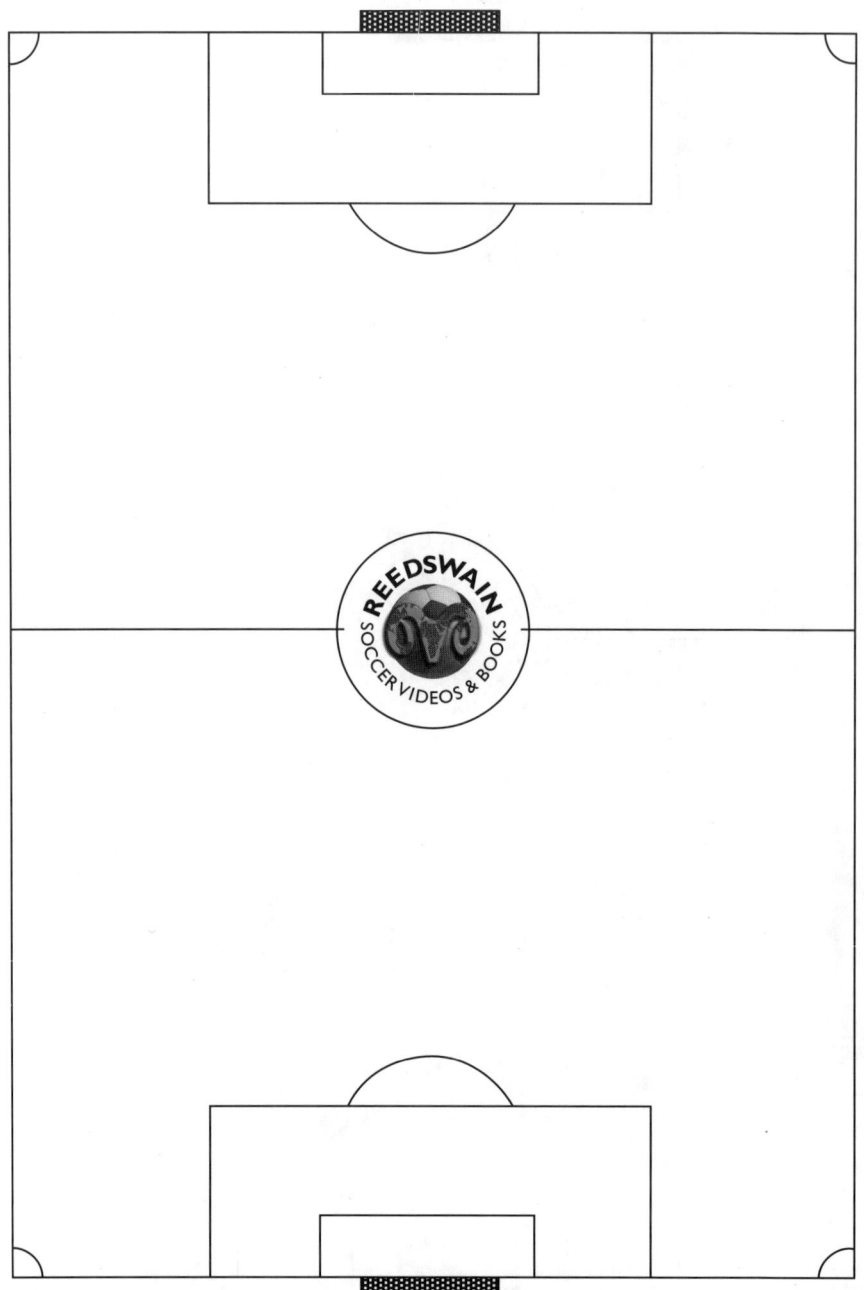

REEDSWAIN INC
612 Pughtown Road
Spring City, Pennsylvania 19475
1-800-331-5191 • www.reedswain.com